THE BREATH
THE ESSENCE OF THE SPIRITUAL TRADITION

RUAH • PNEUMA • SPIRITUS • QI • KI • PRANA • RUH

MICHEL **CHIAMBRETTO**

Discovery Publisher

First published in French:
Le Souffle sous le sceau du secret, 2013, Mercure Dauphinois

For the English edition:
2025, ©Discovery Publisher, Michel Chiambretto
All rights reserved

No part of this book may be reproduced in any form or by any electronic or mechanical means including information storage and retrieval systems, without permission in writing from the publisher.

Author: Michel Chiambretto
Translator (French to English): Vladimir Markov

616 Corporate Way
Valley Cottage, New York
www.discoverypublisher.com
editors@discoverypublisher.com
Proudly not on Facebook or Twitter

New York • Paris • Dublin • Tokyo • Hong Kong

Table of Contents

Foreword	7
The Nature of the Breath	11
The Nature of the "Self"	27
The Influence of the Subjective	43
Static and Dynamic Religion	53
Esoteric Texts	69
Excursion on the Illusory Byways	81
The State of Mind to Strive For	91
The Tools	99
In Conclusion	119
Bibliography	131

THE BREATH
THE ESSENCE OF THE
SPIRITUAL TRADITION

RUAH • PNEUMA • SPIRITUS • QI • KI • PRANA • RUH

MICHEL **CHIAMBRETTO**

DISCLAIMER

The author and the publisher are not responsible for any injury resulting from the practice of instructions included in this book. The described activities, physical or other, could be tiresome or dangerous for certain individuals and so the reader should consult a medical professional beforehand.

The author and the publisher do not recommend nor approve self-treatment by laymen in this matter, and cannot be held responsible for treatments done on the basis of information contained in this book.

Drawings: Rémy, Max, Michel.

My thanks to Claudine, Marie, Paul, Thomas, Didier, Vlad.

And also to H.M. Chan Buddhist monk, Masters W.X.J. and W.S.W. of the Chinese internal tradition, Roman Catholic Prior Don M., L.B.-M. Yoga Master, A.F. Master of the Occult, the F.: H.A., S.B., C.C., G.M., and Xue Yuan Kong Jin.

The illusion ends with the death of the illusionist.

M.C.

Foreword

A topic such as "the Breath[1]"—or "spiritual energy"—can only be of interest to a person on a quest: a quest for truth, authenticity, a different relation, a discovery of an absolute beyond any understanding.

These days one has to be atypical to start on this path, which has no material gain in view. A path that promises neither power, nor appearance, nor profit, but simply a possibility to bring an answer to the *extreme thirst* coming from one's Profound[2] that no one and nothing can quench. A *thirst* present within since forever and which progressively has become so pervasive that it requires a total involvement.

This book proposes a path to follow, providing indications on the direction to be taken, the steps to be made, the battle to be lead. It will provide details that will allow you to refine your discernment of the traditions covered, by keeping you informed of the mistakes and illusions to avoid; that is to say, the *illusory byways* intended for the greatest number of people, or in short, the exoteric approach. Above all, it will give you the ability to "recognize" the authentic methods of work that can open your mind toward a real and concrete awareness of the "Breath". This "Breath" can become matter and can be transformed, with time and effort, and a certain level of abnegation,

---

1. Often translated as "energy": the origin of this "translation/interpretation" comes undoubtedly from Henri Bergson's: *Spiritual Energy: Essays and Lectures, 1919 (texts and conferences published between 1901 and 1913)*, even though it was actually described as "spiritual energy".
The term "energy", which appears more "concrete" to the layman, has been kept because it "sells better". To simplify reading, the author will only use the term "breath" in quotation marks to express the "breath/spiritual energy".

2. By the "Profound" the author means the transcendent spiritual dimension hidden inside every individual. To be distinguished from the "profound" or "deep": the Limbic system or Reptilian brain, i.e. the unconscious.

into a link allowing the Union.

When reading the previous lines, the logical question that comes to mind is:

"Why reveal the principles of a "Tool[1]" that has always been considered a "secret"?"

This is also something we asked ourselves before writing this essay. Our answer was based on:

- Firstly, the "contemporary deviation". Today, most seminars dedicated to learning spiritual methods or exercises have a common mercantile character, despite their diversity. The resulting merchandising system, targeted at certain social categories, offers a sophisticated ritual, a flattering individuation, a culture to embrace, a language to adopt, all with the theoretical aim of assimilating the *"tools"* on offer. The whole rests on the supports of the ego, such as the desire for extraordinary knowledge, power and, most of all, appearance. Which can only prevent the *"tools"* from working, at least the authentic ones.

- In view of the above, two attitudes are possible: either one resigns oneself and accepts the nature of things and people, or one decides, for one last time, to throw a stone in the river, hoping that the ripples will move in a direction away from the common one. There are sincere Seekers who waste precious time in philosophical and intellectual research, while following a progression of elaborate rituals. Over time, they see their impetus fade, as they begin to realize that what they are doing is not working, and that only the illusion of appearances has been satisfied. Consequently, and in the interest of the Tradition itself, our duty to act as a "bridge" becomes self-evident.

With this in mind, this book aims to highlight the importance of the "Breath" in the various Traditions of the East, Far East and West. In these different latitudes, all authentic Traditions indicate that the "Breath" is the primordial element for connecting with God, the Tao, the All, although the metaphors and parables used need to be deciphered.

Last but not least, this book intends to emphasize something that must become obvious at some point. Something that will lead you to *"progres-*

---

1. By "Tool" the author means the "method" allowing to achieve a widening of the field of consciousness — for example: prayer, meditation, contemplation, pranayama, etc.

sively accept to enter the sea, then to continue until there is no foothold, while learning how to swim, and lastly to consent to drown[1]*."*

As can be seen, the path is the reverse of contemporary spiritual traditions, be they esoteric or initiatory, and what they offer, to wit, a construct of knowledge, rituals, techniques, attires and attractive novel cultures. The means are always the same: presenting the product as exceptional, offering the possibility to augment one's potential in various rewarding areas and above all offering to differentiate oneself from the ordinary. Of course, it can be said that in order to attract the layman rattles have to be waved, otherwise no one will be interested, or very few. This is true, however it always ends up in total confusion—with time, the mantle of the Seeker thickens and it becomes impossible for him to "present himself naked".

> *For this reason Bergson, philosopher of consciousness, divides religion into two: static religion and dynamic religion*[2]*.*
>
> *The former has a societal function, defining prohibitions and taboos through dogma, in contrast to the latter, which has for objective human fulfillment.*
>
> *This same confusion was highlighted by René Guénon, who noted that Islam presents primitive Christianity as "Tariqa" (initiatory path), and not as "Sharia" (social legislation), thus demonstrating the evolution of an initiatory message toward a moral path understandable by all and so intended for the greatest number of people*[3]*. An evolution that can be considered generic to contemporary religious, esoteric and initiatory fields.*

Our purpose is the opposite. It consists in showing you the elements necessary for the personal transmutation necessary for embarking on a path of initiation. This transformation will not happen by adding new stones to one's "inner temple", which in this case can only be an egocentric construct, but through a progressive deconstruction in order to find one's inner essence.

"I will destroy this house, and none shall be able to build it again."[4]

This is an extremely difficult task. It is necessary not only to gain awareness of one's conditioning, but also to confront one's nature, even the deep

---

1. A metaphor used by the author, which is relevant to any authentic spiritual path.
2. Henri Bergson, *The two sources of morality and religion*, University of Notre Dame Press, 1977
3. Jean Marc Vivenza, *Le dictionnaire de René Guénon*, Le Mercure Dauphinois, 2002
4. Gospel of Thomas 71

instinct that encloses every human in a bubble of consciousness.

For this reason, this book is not ordered in a logical or reasonable way. It may appear chaotic, but rest assured that at the end of this reading, a part of your deep "self" will feel impacted provided, of course, that you "open up" a little. In fact, this book is not addressed at the intellect but at the Other. The Other[1], who talks to us from time to time. The one who has been all but erased during our early childhood, when we were told by education that our thoughts are wrong, that our feelings do not conform, that what we perceive is the fruit of imagination or does not exist, that we have to join the world of adults.

Therefore, what follows should be read without preconceived ideas, without accepting or rejecting what is written. Simply read with a peaceful mind, same as a long, tranquil river follows its course, meandering its way through the twists and turns, and finally returning to its sea of origin.

No promises of superiority, of happiness with a capital H, of improved health, of potential performance. No, only the promise of rediscovering a long lost sense, so that one day, perhaps, you can become One by communing with the "undifferentiated breath", if God opens the door for you, if the Tao welcomes you, if you awaken.

Ready to continue?

Let us walk together for a while...

---

1. *"He now has become myself whom before I called "Another!""*
Kabir, introduction and translation from Hindi and notes by Charlotte Vaudeville, Oxford: Clarendon Press, 1974

The Nature of the Breath

It is possible to find its trace under all latitudes, in most authentic traditions, whether religious, esoteric, mesoteric or exoteric, even philosophical ones. Of course, to recognize it, it is necessary to know the etymology of the different names used, as well as the meaning of the many parables and metaphors.

Faced with this multiplicity, the very notion has often found itself divided into multiple concepts, or even imaginary abstractions, confusing any and all understanding of the initial meaning and consequently of the initiatory dimension contained within.

If we list the different words that express the "Breath" today, we find:

- *Rua* in Hebrew
- *Pneuma* in Greek
- *Spiritus* in Latin
- *Ruh* in Arabic
- *Qi (Chi)* in Chinese
- *Ki* in Japanese
- *Prana* in Sanskrit

However, the list would be incomplete without taking into account the notion of "the holder of the breath within oneself" in the sense of "soul breath", "breath-self", "animated breath", "differentiated breath", or:

- *Nephesh* in Hebrew
- *Psukhe* in Greek
- *Anima* in Latin

- *An-Nafs* in Arabic
- *Hun* in Chinese
- *Atman* in Sanskrit

Lastly, to conclude this list, the fundamental texts of these religions also mention it using terms such as: wind, spirit, life, breath of life, the animated, the soul, the Holy Spirit, Angel Gabriel, inhale, exhale, breathing, impetus.

Some examples, chronologically:

- **In Brahmanism** *(about 1500 years BC)*, we find in the *Upanishads (reference texts)* the notion of Atman *(breath/soul)*, considered as the deepest essence of man.

The Atman is the breath of life at the origin of creation. It is buried deep within every human being, and constitutes the consciousness-carrying soul, the conscious self.

> *"In Prana all things that we see around us [moving or unmoving], disappear [at the time of their destruction. And at the time of their appearance,] they appear from Prana.[1]"*

But this self-awareness, which is also the link with the divine, can join the *Brahman*, the individual soul merging with the universal soul. However, this union cannot be described with words, because it is experiential.

The *Prana (material or immaterial breath)* for its part, is born from the Atman whose seat is in the heart.

"This Prana is born from Atman.[2]"

It is one of the five breaths of the body and by circulating connects the eyes, ears, mouth and nose.

The work of *Pranayama* in Yoga *(control or retention of the breath)* is therefore a part of this tradition. *Atman* is no longer mentioned today in the West, probably in order not to relate to Brahmanism.

Authentic *Pranayama (and Yoga techniques in general)* is not intended to be a physiological massage, to declog the body or invigorate antibodies, but to connect the Atman to the Brahman, the individual breath to the cosmic

---

1. *Chandogya Upanishad (1.11.5)*, translated by Swami Lokeswarananda, Ramakrishna Math, 1998
2. *Prashna Upanishad (3.3)*, translated by Swami Sivananda

breath, in awareness, as is the case in any authentic tradition.

- **In Taoism** *(6th century BC)* the "breath" is also a connecting element, of relation between the self and the *Tao*. Knowing that the two are dissociated only by our awareness of the "moment".

Lao Tzu (Laozi) says about the Tao[1]:

"How still it was and formless, standing alone, and undergoing no change, reaching everywhere and in no danger (of being exhausted)! It may be regarded as the Mother of all things."

"Profound it is, dark and obscure;

Things' essences all there endure.

Those essences the truth enfold…"

And about humans:

"All things leave behind them the Obscurity (out of which they have come), and go forward to embrace the Brightness (into which they have emerged), while they are harmonized by the Breath of Vacancy."

Tao did not originally mean "Way" as contemporary translations interpret it, but rather, as Henri Borel notes:

"From the symbolism of Tao's character itself, it naturally follows that it was not a question of path or way, but of Head, of the very Principle that circulates in the Universe[2]."

Which is obvious in the *Tao Te Ching* of Lao Tzu[3]:

"The Tao, considered as unchanging, has no name."

"The Tao is hidden, and has no name;"

"I do not know its name, and I give it the designation of the Tao."

"The Tao is hidden, and has no name…"

Chuang Tzu (Zhuang Zhou, Zhuangzi, 4th century BC) recalls when talking about his dead wife:

"When she first died, I certainly mourned just like everyone else! However, I

---

1. *The sacred books of the East (The Tao Teh King)*, translated by James Legge, 1891
2. Henri Borel, *L'esprit de la Chine*, La main courante, 2007
3. *The sacred books of the East (The Tao Teh King)*, translated by James Legge, 1891

then thought back to her birth and to the very roots of her being, before she was born. Indeed, not just before she was born but before the time when her body was created. Not just before her body was created but before the very origin of her life's breath. Out of all of this, through the wonderful mystery of change she was given her life's breath.[1]"

Chu Hsi (Zhu Xi, 12th century AD) describes the change of state:

"When Taï breathed for the first time, this ethereal, actually coagulated breath, generated the Yang, and when this breath had reached the extreme point, and Taï had regained the state of rest, he generated the Yin[2]."

To conclude on the Taoist tradition, we would like to remind that the Taoist work of *inner alchemy* is based on the notions of *Jing*, *Qi (breath)* and *Shen*. Concepts that will be explained later.

- **In Buddhism** *(6th century BC)* the notion of "breath" is also essential. Today, however, we can see that it has remained a very discreet teaching.

Indeed, it is quite surprising to see that the notion of "breathing" is limited entirely to physiological breathing for most contemporary currents of this tradition, at least when interpreted for the layman. Nonetheless, the Lotus position, which helps the feet to open up to the "subtle breath" (and the same goes for the palms, the belly breathing and the tip of the tongue pressed to the roof of the mouth), is proof to the contrary. The principles of "conscious breathing" specific to certain schools are just as much a matter of precise work (*a Tool*) with the "breath", and this even if renowned *"specialists"* say that:

"The right state of mind flows naturally from deep concentration on physical posture and breathing. The one with breath lives long, intensely, peacefully. The correct exercise of breath makes it possible to neutralize nervous shocks, to manage instincts and passions, and to control mental activity."

In contrast to this exoteric approach intended for the masses, the esoteric dimension of the "Breath" is only intended for Seekers on a quest, as Shakyamuni confirms:

"And I discovered that profound truth, so difficult to perceive, difficult to understand, tranquillizing and sublime, which is not to be gained by mere

---

1. *The book of Chuang Tzu*, translated by Martin Palmer, Penguin Classics, 2006
2. Henri Borel, ibidem

reasoning, and is visible only to the wise.[1]"

However, it may also be a question of formulation, as the boundary between "pure consciousness" and "Breath" fades on its own, as we will discuss later. It can also be said that without "Breath" any emptiness could only be, as stated by Chan Buddhism, "stubborn emptiness[2]".

As an example of work with the "Breath", we can mention the attention directed to breathing and then to the thirty-two parts of the body of the *Sutta-pitaka, (oral teachings of Buddha transcribed in the 1st century),* as well as the attention linked to the counting of breaths of the *Visuddhimagga ("The Path of Purity",* 430 AD) of Buddhaghosa. Unfortunately, this "tool" is often seen in the West as a method using the physiological breathing to calm and focus the mind, which is certainly due to a lack of awareness/perception of the "matter" to be worked on *("the breath" must be "matter", otherwise how to sculpt the wind?).*

Another example is the Buddhist mantra *(tool of the Spirit)* which is exemplary for those who have been introduced to its use. Its principle is the repetition of a sound and rhythmic formula with the purpose of guiding the "breath".

But it is true that the mantra is often presented as a "magic" formula to the layman, the latter not possessing, in awareness, the necessary "matter".

Such "magic" is in opposition to the principles of the Buddha:

"It is because I see danger in the practice of these mystic wonders that I loathe and abhor and am ashamed thereof.[3]"

In the Tibetan tradition, a demonstrative expression of sound linked to the "Breath" is made by means of polyphonic chants, called *dbyangs ("vowels" in Tibetan)*, where two to three notes are simultaneously emitted.

Finally, we can also mention the mudras, which are not a *"codified and symbolic positioning of the hands"*, but rather a principle of closing one of the "Breath" circuits, so as to provoke a particular opening of consciousness.

---

1. Nyanatiloka (compiler, translator), *The Word of the Buddha: An Outline of the Teaching of the Buddha in the Words of the Pali Canon*, 14th edition, Buddhist Publication Society, 1967
2. Dalai Lama and Sheng Yen, *Meeting of minds*, Dharma Drum Publications, 1999
3. Dīgha Nikāya

And to further emphasize the importance of the "breath" in this tradition, it is worth pointing out that when Buddhism made its first incursion into China in the 2nd century, the Taoist Masters of the time said that it was *"identical to original Taoism"*.

- **In Christianity**, the "Breath" is often described as the "Holy Spirit" of the *"Trinitarian Mystery" (Father, Son, Holy Spirit)*.

The transcriptions are: *Ruah* in Hebrew, *Pneuma* in Greek and *Spiritus* in Latin, often translated as *"breath", "spirit", "breathing", "wind", "Holy Spirit"*. *Ruah* is quoted more than three hundred times in the Bible.

To mention but a few examples of the use of the word "Breath":

◊ In the Book of Genesis:

  * Chapter II

"Then the Lord God formed a man from the dust of the ground and breathed into his nostrils the breath of life, and the man became a living being."

  * Chapter VI

"I am going to bring floodwaters on the earth to destroy all life under the heavens, every creature that has the breath of life in it."

  * Psalm 33:6

"By the word of the Lord the heavens were made, their starry host by the breath of his mouth."

  * Proverbs 20:27

"The human spirit is the lamp of the Lord that sheds light on one's inmost being."

◊ In the Gospel according to Saint John 3:8:

"The wind blows wherever it pleases. You hear its sound, but you cannot tell where it comes from or where it is going. So it is with everyone born of the Spirit."

Saint Paul contrasted the spiritual person *(pneumatikos)* with the psychic person *(psuchikos,* who has no Spirit).

  * 1st Corinthians 2:14

"The person without the Spirit does not accept the things that come from the

Spirit of God but considers them foolishness, and cannot understand them because they are discerned only through the Spirit."

Christian Gnostics took up this opposition, distinguishing between *"hylics"* (those attached to matter), *"psychics"* (Christians, but cut off from the Truth), and *"pneumatics"* (those who have the Knowledge, who possess Gnosis).

It should also be noted that nowadays work with the "Breath" is more particularly present in the Greek Orthodox tradition.

- **In Islam**, "Breath" is written as *"Ruh"* in the Quran.

Its different meanings are: "Breath of Life", "Holy Spirit" or "Angel Gabriel" who is the Intermediary for the *"Word of God"* (Revelation of the Quran).

Ruh is mentioned more than twenty times in the Quran. Some examples:

* Ali 'Imran 3:49

"I have come to you with a sign from your Lord: I will make for you a bird from clay, breathe into it, and it will become a real bird—by Allah's Will."

* An-Nisa 4:171

"O People of the Book! Do not go to extremes regarding your faith; say nothing about Allah except the truth. The Messiah, Jesus, son of Mary, was no more than a messenger of Allah and the fulfillment of His Word through Mary and a spirit 'created by a command' from Him."

* Al-Hijr 15:29

"So when I have fashioned him and had a spirit of My Own creation breathed into him, fall down in prostration to him."

* Al-Waqi'ah 56:83

"Why then are you helpless when the soul of a dying person reaches their throat..." (of a moribund)

The esoteric current of Islam, *"Sufism"*, presents a fascinating work with the breath using to the following tools:

◊ *Dhikr,* "remembrance of Allah", which consists in repeating the name of God with a particular intention linked to the "Breath", accompanied in some cases by mental attention to certain points of the body.

And we should not forget:

◊ *Sama,* "dance" of the whirling Derviches of the Mevlevi Sufis whose aesthetic aspect hides not only a great symbolism, but also a connection with *palpable* "Breath" for those who are aware of the "Breath" (not to be confused with the parodies offered to tourists).

As these few examples demonstrate, the notion of "Breath" is universal. It appears to always be:

- at the origin of human life,
- the link that ties humans to this origin,
- that which maintains their existence.

At some point every Seeker becomes aware that this notion unites all spiritual traditions, bearing witness to the existence of a "Primordial Tradition[1]", common to all mankind.

What is more, while in contact with discreet, esoteric and initiatory brotherhoods emanating from these different traditions, the Seeker discovers that the purpose of the tools provided in confidence is work with this "Breath" *(except when the "Breath" has become an "abstraction").*

Most of the time the answer the Seeker is given on the interest of such practices is that they make it possible to amplify the "Breath" and therefore the relation with God, Allah, the Father, the Holy Spirit, the Tao, the All, the One, as each tradition wishes to translate it.

It is necessary for any sincere Seeker to approach the mystery of the "Breath" and, to do so, to know its nature. The first step would be for him to look at his own conditioning. But, as a consequence of the education received, like all his peers, to understand the new element he will begin with its definition. He will consult books and dictionaries on esoteric topics. Once obtained, the details and explanations provided will bring the desired conceptual satisfaction, which would be the result of an analysis made by the "Knowledgeables[2]", chosen by society for their intellectual qualities.

---

1. Primordial tradition: meaning the one transmitted since the dawn of time, universal by the nature of man.
2. Knowledgeable: "man of knowledge", where knowledge is in the realm of the intellect, in contrast with Seeker, "a man on a quest", realm of the experiential

Then, having filed said "element" in a drawer of his memory, the understanding of the budding Seeker will be, from then on, limited to the learned definition. This is true to such an extent, that even in modern so-called "initiatory" associations, any essay begins with dictionary definitions, and paradoxically, this remains true even when the topic in question is a symbol.

A contemporary paradox—rather than escaping the rut of the definition through work with the symbol, the recipient finds himself forced back into it by the dictionary he is using.

What are the consequences of such "lapses"?

They are dramatic. Indeed, everything is restricted to the learned definition, and therefore any personal inquiry can only be done within a pre-defined limit. There is confusion between intellectual analysis, i.e. Reason[1] *(the cortex)* and the intuitive approach of the deep brains.

As a result of this type of conditioning, any individual perception is delimited by imposed criteria, or differently put, by the writings of society's recognized intellectuals. This is an important, or rather fundamental, point because any sensitive perception is, in fact, modified, channeled.

Accordingly, to escape this hold, it is essential to approach the notion of "Breath" not with definitions, but by first listing what it is not. We will first list the pitfalls that the layman encounters most frequently.

These pitfall traps are all the more effective because they originate, for some, from religious currents that are supposed to bring *"the good word"*, or from esoteric movements that represent the most publicized paths of initiation or awakening. This causes great confusion in the mind of the Seeker who, respecting the societal order, is unable to question the philosophical-religious analyses offered by the institutional elites.

It is necessary to note that any expression of *"dynamic religion"* must involve the reality of *"being connected"*, and that the "esoteric" domain corresponds to knowledge *"hidden from ordinary people"*. These two universes are linked by experience, that is, by an opening of a previously hidden field of consciousness. The latter is a new perception not achievable by an up-front reasoned approach, since it is totally inconceivable by the intellect, and in

---

1. Reason: the entirety of the intellectual faculties allowing to discern true from false, good from bad, and organizing one's relation with reality

fact not definable, because it is located outside any reference.

It should be pointed out that, depending on the stage reached, this "opening" can be equated to a new sense. Without it, it is all quibbling.

Chan Buddhism provides some examples such as:

"How to describe pain to someone who has never felt it?"

There is a difference between "knowledge", which is at the level of the intellect, and "knowing", which is in the experiential realm, and therefore at the level of the sensitive. Alexandra David-Néel called it "transcendent knowing".

It is not a question of developing a beautiful, refined theory and then selling it with self-aggrandizing promises that will make the ego salivate with envy. This is always useful to remember to avoid being trapped in the usual sales schemes of the esoteric and pseudo-religious New Age.

Not to mention that such traps have been around since the dawn of time. Lao Tzu, the old Taoist sage, said 600 years BC:

"True words are not pleasing. Pleasing words are not true."

Further confirmed by Hui Neng, patriarch of Chan Buddhism, in the 8th century:

"The ignorant person practices seeking future happiness, and does not practice the Way, and says that to practice seeking future happiness is the Way.[1]"

The above should raise questions about the various promises of Happiness, Paradise, Nirvana, Awakening in bliss, "suffering that goes away", "better health", healing, charisma, power, etc. Promises offered to the public since the dawn of time. Although they may be useful in attracting the butterfly.

Now, let us address the pitfalls that the Seeker has to avoid.

- First of all, the most common one, which consists in being satisfied with the interpretation of metaphors according to the dogma.

  This is a mould, which cannot be disposed of. Everything has been dissected, explained, defined. Everything must be in its place and nothing can be moved. The dogma is the guarantor of Truth, there is no other possible interpretation. Moreover, in the event of slip-ups, there are

---

1. Hui Neng, *The Platform Sutra of the Sixth Patriarch,* Columbia University Press, 1967, p. 154

multiple possible sanctions, whether of moral or divine nature.

As understanding escapes the human dimension, it therefore must be admitted as an inaccessible Truth. As a result, the intuitive cannot be "touched", because the postulated impenetrable aspect only leads to a passive state. The answers are provided, no need whatsoever to take the experiential path — *this can be true in both monotheistic and more philosophical religions, such as Buddhism or Taoism. In each of them, the doctrine in place can limit any approach.*

Admitting that the "Breath" is beyond one's level of understanding, opening up to the unknown, does not always seem possible, one may "lose one's footing". One's entire construction would be called into question and the ensuing emotion would only lead to a profound ill-being. To avoid this, the solution is to use the Doctrine to develop a theory about the given topic. The ground is stable, walked by all, and no one is shaken; "all is for the best in the best of possible worlds."

In addition, at the Limbic level, the unconscious desire not to be rejected by the group is at work. For the ego, the desire to demonstrate to oneself and to others that one understands everything, that one is not *out of one's depth*, is a complementary motivation.

- The second pitfall, just as frequent, is the intellectualization of the texts of reference. Understanding of the "*Breath*" and its interpretations is sought through didactic and discursive methods.

One paradox to highlight, which we will cover in detail later, is that breathing can be used as a support for work with the "Breath". Moreover, it is worth pointing out that in the early stages, the "Breath" is perceived as a sensation, like breathing through the body, hence why the term "Breath".

This second pitfall leads to two possible outcomes:

- The first is practiced by "scholars", who use their cortex as their tool of choice and text analysis as their main method. This involves examining the various works on the topic, dissecting their content within the limits of the translation, of the historical and societal contexts, while taking into account the theological and philosophical knowledge acquired. The selected texts are then compared on these bases, similarities are detailed and contradictions highlighted.

An intellectually stimulating work, even exciting in some cases, but limited to the intellect.

- The second outcome is the method commonly adopted by self-taught pseudo-seekers, or those educated in traditions that have lost their roots.

The recipe consists in combining excerpts from the various texts read, and then using those to produce a set of theories that align with the desires of the pseudo-seeker; which is particularly useful for merchandising purposes *(product enhancement)*. This is the most frequently used method today, and most published texts are designed this way. It is hardly surprising, then, that the "self-awakened" and "self-initiated" of many modern currents are the product of an intellectual construction.

This type of approach remains the most attractive for the layman because it is entirely didactic, based on references that already exist in him. And so it is the ultimate trap.

- The third pitfall we will mention (knowing that the list cannot be exhaustive) is to think that the "Breath" is an "abstraction", a fruit of the imagination.

Such an interpretation of the "Breath" is the result of an extreme materialistic conditioning. Anything that escapes "my" perception cannot exist, according to the precept of Saint Thomas who wanted to see the scars of the nails to believe in the resurrection *(which is far removed from the metaphors in the Gospel of Thomas; not a first degree of understanding: seeing is believing, but an allegory: seeing the nails means approaching the spiritual realm through experience, not with theories; only experience can provide an answer)*.

This rejection of that which is "not perceived by the senses", or "not accepted by society", or "not proven by science", is the mark of a rationality that can be an asset and an obstacle at the same time:

- *Obstacle*, because, as we will see, it blocks any future progress. "*How to open up to an unsuspected perception if from the outset one refuses any possibility of entering the unknown?*" Having established as dogma that it does not exist, the mind will be "stone" and one's consciousness will be closed to any possibility other than the one set as a limit; all the result of an effective self-conditioning. This is not that different from the observance of religious dogma, the two extremes meeting, the dogma of the atheist and that of the believer.

- *Asset*, because not imagining a "programmed sequence" avoids settling into a mental illusion and, above all, avoids "*delimiting freedom*" of perception, which may be considered a dead end in any spiritual quest (but can be observed in many sectarian groups).

Knowing how to use the positive side of this paradox, approaching the unknown with what will be offered at the level of one's experience as one's only reference, "the experiential realm", is an asset in this endeavor.

To complete our list of potential pitfalls, we should also mention the contemporary merchandising trend that uses the term "energy" *(a translation originally particular to the West)* to sell the "Breath". Indeed, what could be more profitable than offering an "energy" that can bring health, vitality, strength and beauty, or even a magical spiritual link?

This craze comes in part from the modern currents of Chi Kung (Qigong), Tai Chi (Taijiquan), Feng Shui, Tao Yin, Taoist, Indian, Tibetan Yoga, Yang Sheng, Reiki, etc., which all promise the above and even much more.

We will describe the essential differences between the authentic Tradition of these teachings and the modern exercises in a following chapter. This is all the more important since these contemporary trends are a reflection of the mistakes in the working principles not to be committed.

It should be noted that *Prana* in Yoga is victim of the same popularity as Chi *(Qi, Ki)* and accordingly of the same translation. The term "energy" is not neutral because it is understood according to the learned definition, and therefore seen as being able to make one more efficient, to produce more strength, to allow one to be in full health, or less sick, in other words to be "more than oneself" or "more than others". "*Energy, energy, are you there?*" thus becoming the leitmotiv of the type of work on offer.

And this resonates well with the contemporary individual who is facing the issues of a society in search of energy that is scarce; oil, gas, coal… Indeed, touching on the unconscious concerns instilled by the media, means that the gurus of the supra-sensory, themselves, as well as their potential customers, are receptive to the term "energy". That is how it is, but everyone is free to interpret things differently[1].

---

1. Only Aristotle's approach, which specifies that energy represents "actual reality, as opposed to potential reality" appears correct, but is less marketable.

However, let us ask ourselves the following question: would this term have had the same impact a few centuries earlier? Can we translate *Ruah, Spiritus, Pneuma, Ruh,* as energy? This has never been the case. Yet many points of convergence are to be noted: the *Qi* or *Ki* is the original breath, it connects all things and beings, it encompasses the entire universe, it is the "undifferentiated breath" of the Tao.

A recurring problem for many Seekers is that their research is focused on the apparent differences between existing traditions instead of examining their common points, the connections, the very essence at their origin. Moreover, Chinese Internal Alchemy *(Neidan, Deng Yuzhi (483–493) then the Tang dynasty (618–907))*[1] expresses *Qi* with a notion of breath such as *Yuan qi (original or primal breath)*, or *Zhen qi (true or median breath)*[2].

It is this concept of energy that makes the illusionists of the New Age declare: "I feel this energy in me!", "I perceive it, I feel it in the other!", "I see the energy that is emitted by… ", "I can emit it through my hands" *(without any work on the Profound)*, "I can heal.", etc. and thus inflate my ego and sell my know-how (this obviously does not mean that the "Breath" cannot be used to heal, by some very rare and exceptional people, who are in communion with the "primordial Breath").

One could laugh it off, if it were not unbearable for those following the path, limiting the spiritual realm to another materialistic, even blasphemous good.

> *"He who blasphemes against the Father will be forgiven, and he who blasphemes against the Son will be forgiven; but he who blasphemes against the Holy Spirit will not be forgiven, either on earth or in heaven.*[3]*"*

In the exotic realm of Chinese, Japanese, Indian, Celtic, Nepalese, Tibetan and other body and soul therapies, so-called energy arts, so-called martial arts, as well as wellness treatments on sale, the term "energy" sells and makes customers dream of differentiation and of surpassing themselves.

As we can see, the dead-ends are numerous, to say the least. The question

---

1. The earliest known Chinese alchemical treatise is the Baopuzi Neipian written by Ge Hong (283-343 AD)
2. Muriel Baryosher-Chemouny, *La Quête de l'immortalité en Chine*, Éditions Dervy, 1996
3. Gospel of Thomas 44

that arises then is:

"*So, where and how to look for this "Breath"?*

This is the purpose of this book. As promised, we are going to take you part of the way on the road to knowledge of the "Breath".

But first we need to get rid of the superfluous!

The Nature of the "Self"

What is this superfluous thing that we must rid ourselves of?

To go towards the "Profound", which is the only possible link with the "Breath", it is necessary to know oneself, not one's personality, at least not yet, but the different layers that cover one's essential being.

It could be argued that this is unnecessary, that this is what the Tool is for. Which would be right and wrong at the same time:

- Right because without the tool's work, it would be nothing more than an interesting intellectual analysis, of little to no practical use.
- Wrong for several reasons:

    - First, *"to find water, one has to start digging to detect moisture that was not on the surface"*. Once detected, it can only stir up "thirst" conducive to the search.

    - Second, the person who is going to use the tool, i.e. the budding Seeker, is covered in a heavy mantle. To begin "dismantling" this "cover" over one's essential Being is desirable from the outset. But first one has to be aware of its presence!

    - Finally, the most important one. The inner fight that takes place as one moves along the path, and the subsequent destabilization caused by one's own deconstruction, make it necessary to set up a "role-playing game" to adapt to the ambient mould, in order to not harm those around. This is essential, to say the least. First and foremost, then, the future actor needs to know what is the role assigned to him in society.

So let us start peeling the layers.

The embryo is in the mother's womb, growing. During that time, is it influenced by the mother, her emotions, her feelings, everything she ingests and experiences? The answer seems obvious. What is more, does not the initial state of every being allow it to empathically perceive any life in proximity? It is conceivable. It is possible that Adam and Eve's exit from paradise after tasting the fruit of the Tree of Good and Evil is an allegory for the newborn baby. This baby, whatever the species, human or animal, is not yet fully invested by its specific nature. Nature proper to the species, followed progressively by the sexual temperament, all of which gradually veils one's essence and the qualities associated with it. Then, over time, as a result of the mould imposed by society and the immediate environment, this essence is further masked from the conscious mind, as if wrapped in layers, a heavy mantle covering it. This would suggest that the "thirst" at the root of the Seeker's quest is due to a crack in this envelope. A bit like a cracked clay vase that allows water to ooze out, the moisture on the surface provoking the thirst. The Tool, meanwhile, enables the Seeker to work on breaking the vase, echoing Kabir's metaphor.

"Take a pitcher full of water and set it down in the water—now it has water inside and water outside.[1]"

From this rupture emerges that which is buried deep within us, our essence, the "breath". Some vases are cracked, others not; some are sincere Seekers, others not. It is a question of nature and not individual "will", so there can be no pretenses.

Two new questions may then arise:

- "Can a violent emotional shock crack the vase?"
- "But is this the case for speculative work on the nature of man?"

As for the first question, there is testimonial evidence to support this. As for the second one, it appears legitimate, thanks to our intellectual education, but it is not a real possibility, because the intellect *(the Neocortex)* cannot affect the "Profound", which is what we are now discussing.

Let us continue.

The child has grown up. He now has his human nature and his sexual nature. What does this mean?

Here we will discuss Paul D. MacLean's theory[2] of the triune brain, later

---

1. Moatty (Yves), *Kabir: le fils de Ram et d'Allah*, Éditions Les deux Océans, 1988
2. Paul D. MacLean, *The Triune Brain in Evolution: Role in Paleocerebral Functions*, Plenum, 1990

taken up by Henri Laborit. Even though today the hypothesis of the evolution of the human brain in three distinct stages developed by these neurobiologists is contested, the schematic of its functional organization, on the other hand, appears to be quite precise. Indeed, the principles contained in the theory are used in fields as varied as marketing, manager training, personal development, mentalism, martial arts and spirituality.

These three brains would have appeared progressively during the evolution of our species: reptiles, then mammals— *the first mammals; humans are mammals with a developed Neocortex*— to arrive at the *exceptional* beings that we are. Exceptional in this case meaning "unusual" and not necessarily "wonderful". Or, three superimposed brains: the reptilian *(cerebral trunk)*, the mammalian—(paleomammalian, Limbic system), the Neocortex (neomammalian, intellect).

Their respective functions can be broken down as follows:

- **The Reptilian** is the "primitive" brain, found in reptiles, birds, fish. Its main function is survival. It is responsible for homeostasis, that is to say, "*the dynamic balance*" of our bodies, by regulating the heart, breathing, temperature, etc., in short, the vital functions. In the latter, one should not forget drinking, eating, sleeping, and finally, *primary for any species*, reproduction;

- **The Mammalian**, or **Limbic** system, called by Dr. Paul D. MacLean "*the visceral brain of survival*", appeared with the first mammalians. Its function is to be the "*physiological center of emotions*". For Henri Laborit, it is the seat of affection, of the ritual (social or group integration), of convictions, beliefs, motivation, feeling of security and above all, of the long memory;

- **The Neocortex** is particularly well developed in humans. It is the "intellectual" brain, allowing logical reasoning, language, anticipation. Henri Laborit notes that it also makes it possible to create new "*imaginary structures*" and, something that must be emphasized: "*the recognition of the object as an external reality in a given space.*[1]"

The most important follows.

The brain that gives us awareness of our existence, the famous "*Cogito, ergo sum*" ("*I think, therefore I am*") is the Neocortex. Which is to say that

---

1. Henri Laborit, *É loge de la fuite*, É dition Gallimard, 1993

the conscious Self is limited to this brain, but as Henri Laborit indicates:

> *"It does not know what to think or suggest. It does not know and cannot do anything"*, adding that *"the brain does not do anything, its supposed intelligent part is subjected to the primitive one, which decides without the former's opinion.[1]"*

Frustrating for the "self", to say the least least.

To summarize, our Neocortex, which we think we paradoxically control with the Neocortex, depends on the Limbic system, which itself depends on the Reptilian brain. The classic image to represent this principle is that of a ship: the captain is the Reptilian brain, the second in command is the Limbic system, the passenger is the Neocortex, or the "Self".

"But fortunately all this is sprinkled with bursts of heart…"

We can understand why all Traditions, religious (*dynamic*), initiatory or esoteric, have as their goal to influence the Profound. Their only problem, a sizable one, is that the Neocortex (*or, if you prefer, reason, intellect, analysis, speculation, willpower*) can have no influence on the other two, the deep brains. It is this fundamental point that seems to have been forgotten today in the majority of groups working within these Traditions.

The reason is certainly the usual confusion between:

- a *"change from one format to another"*,
- and a *"transformation of the state of being"*.

On this subject, the various manipulative techniques available are in fact based on reactions to stimuli exerted on the deep brains. To avoid falling victim to such stimuli, it is "enough" to be aware of them and to also deprogram them by acting on the deep brains.

Various "techniques" exist allowing to stop reacting to certain stimuli. They are used by the military *(often unknowingly)*, by the intelligence services of certain countries, by "knowledgeable" professional trainers and by discreet circles. They all correspond to a partial reprogramming and should not be confused with a spiritual path, which is an "awakening of the sensitive state in order to connect with the essence"…

This child is growing up.

---

1. *"My American Uncle"*, a film by based on the works of Henri Laborit, 1980

As we have just detailed, its species' nature has taken over. It is worth recalling what Konrad Lorenz said:

> *"The instinctive behavior of animals, humans included, is determined by innate stimuli, not learned ones"*, which he called the *"innate mechanisms triggering behavior.[1]"*

These *rituals* of the Limbic, or unconscious, realm, virtually identical to those of the great apes, will dictate one's instinctive actions and reactions. Only the fear of punishment and rejection by the group *(also imprinted in the Limbic)* to which one belongs, will be able to curb them.

- What are these rituals?

For example, the rituals of territory, seduction, submission, selection, domination, provocation, confrontation[2].

What do they involve?

Some obvious examples from everyday life:

- the ritual of "territory": essential for the animal, to feed, to protect the female, to protect the children. This is expressed in the aggressive reactions of the driver (*car = territory*), in the tribal behavior of supporters, in nationalism, xenophobia, etc.
- seduction: the peacock displaying its plumage, the young man showing his muscles, his beautiful car. The young woman rising on her heels, with clothes highlighting her curves. The politician (*the business leader*) showing his power as an Alpha male does. The young saleswoman smiling, pampering, touching…
- submission: the young wolf rolling on its back and presenting its belly, the young employee lowering his eyes, bending his back, flattering, nodding.
- selection: being more beautiful, stronger, smarter, richer.
- domination: the lion roaring, the young males moving away, the hierarchical superior putting his hand on the employee's shoulder, raising his voice, pumping his chest, laughing out loud. The soldier exhibiting his rank and medals, the civilian his standard of living.

---

1. Developed from: Konrad Lorenz, *Evolution and Modification of Behaviour*
2. Konrad Lorenz, *On Aggression*, Routledge, 2002

- provocation: the gorilla beating its chest, the rugby team doing its Hakka, the thug looking provocatively, revving the engine.

- confrontation: deer competing during the rut, young people fighting on the dance floor, opposition in sports events of all kinds, debating competitions for the elderly.

Many, many other examples can be mentioned, even in so-called "evolved" circles.

Observing and surfing on these behavioral rituals is a very good exercise, but we must not forget that, as soon as emotion takes over, "the natural" returns, unless... We will deal with this later.

Any doubts?

It is enough to fall in love, to have power over an "unbearable" person, to be exasperated by the casual attitude of a "youngster", to realize that we act in the same way, at least if we are honest with ourselves.

Why?

Because any emotional exaltation (*always the Limbic brain*) influences ritual behavior and amplifies it.

Apart from the Limbic brain, this growing child is also dependent on the Reptilian one.

For any human or animal, the Reptilian "decides" for both individual survival and that of the species *(reproduction)*. Not to mention that, in exceptional circumstances, when the individual is "out of his mind", the Reptilian can take full control, thus neutralizing the Neocortex and moving from ritual confrontation on to murder, with only a vague blackout as a remaining memory. The dormant animal has awakened.

Mythology describes this struggle between man and beast in a number of metaphors. The myth of Theseus and the Minotaur is a perfect example.

Going deep inside oneself, through the convolutions of one's brain, through the labyrinth of the initiatory path, to find the animal inside and finally kill it *(the animal instinct)*. A perilous task, because it is almost impossible to find the way back to normal. But thanks to the Ariadne's thread that is Tradition, the return becomes possible. Quite the dream, but perhaps it is conceivable, given time, patience and an authentic Tradition.

But let us get back to this child.

Over time, the sexual function gradually becomes a fundamental element of its life. Its sexual impulses, often hidden under an alibi that the intellect provides, make it look for the ideal man/woman to produce offspring. And what seems to be a personal choice is in fact nothing but an impulse of the Reptilian brain acting for the preservation of the species.

As for the choice of a future partner, male or female, it is again the Reptilian brain that will decide by gauging vitality and physique. Not to mention the Limbic brain which, depending on the surrounding environment, will have defined the canons of the "perfect" man/woman by imposing the format of the moment.

Consequently, the importance of the following criteria will vary:

- vitality, physique (*large and muscular for men in the West, breasts and hips/buttocks for women*),
- beauty (*varies according to cultures*),
- security (*strength and/or financial potential, societal format*).

Different variations can be included of course.

In short:

The child is growing up and unintentionally becoming the product of its species' nature, while believing to be an individual in his own right, autonomous and thinking/acting freely. What the child believes to be dependent on its will is often only a set of deep brain decisions that totally escape its awareness.

This is emphasized by Paul D. MacLean, when explaining that ritual and hierarchical behavior in archaic societies, as well as in modern industrial ones, has a strong Reptilian component. And yet this is only a fraction of the hidden part of the iceberg that will remain for the child to discover if it decides to follow the path to its essence.

Additional "layers" will be created at the level of the Limbic by empirical methods designed to act on this brain.

But it must be said that the "layers" put in place by relatives, society, religion, different esoteric, initiatory and personal development groups, are well-intentioned. Their objective, conscious or unconscious, is to develop the qualities of the recipient in order to allow him the best possible integration within society.

This is a rational approach, the opinion of the majority prevailing over any particular analysis. Thus, its effectiveness is increased tenfold[1].

Firstly, if the child is lucky enough to be in a stable, loving family, it will be able to empathize with the heart qualities of those around. *Otherwise, the first indelible traumas will arise, with their likely neurotic consequences.*

We will stick to the ideal case.

Parents will do everything to make the little child happy. Tales will be read, movies shown, already putting in place the hierarchical structures to be accepted: Kings, Queens, Princes and Princesses, highlighted for their innate, even divine qualities of beauty, grace, magnificence, power. These make even adults dream, where the wedding ceremony is nothing but a copy of such tales. It is amazing how many will admire a Queen in her carriage or swoon in front of a princely wedding even today!

The goal is achieved, the hierarchy is accepted. The King *(or his "image")* is in place, he leads and decides, and this is good; just like in any society where it is necessary to accept the existing structure at some point.

Other tales, nursery rhymes, stories, movies, will provide the child with the moral references necessary for its integration into the community. These will be based on a binary notion of Good and Evil, often of a religious origin. And of course, the Good and moral values will always come out victorious, all according to the idealized foundations of society. The playful formative approach has achieved its pedagogical and socializing goal.

So, humans, like all other gregarious animals, following the same instinct, have the need to integrate their offspring into the community in which they live.

This works quite well. The young age, the relentless repetition, the use of the affective and emotional dimension, allow to quickly impress on the Limbic brain.

---

1. Some, like Jean Giono, have spoken out against this: *"Whatever the mediocre produces, it is a product that appeals to the greatest number of people. It is a certain thing, it has the qualities required by the majority of individuals."*

Of course, it could be retorted that in real life Good and moral values are often flouted, that this type of conditioning creates future victims, prey for social predators, that these references vary according to the culture in place, according to the religion that will be given to the child.

To this it can be replied that all Good People anywhere recognize each other, and that the foundations of all religions advocate respect for others. On the other hand, certain values can differ significantly. For example, the samurai's sense of honor is such that he kills women and children to avoid future vengeance, and even goes as far as committing seppuku for his lord (*this certainly "explains" the horrors of Nanjing during the last World War and the suffering endured by English and American prisoners*). We could also mention the Inquisition of the Middle Ages, which tortured and murdered pseudo heretics in front of crowds that came to attend the show. Or the Calvinist Protestant Reformation which, while opposing Catholicism, did the same by burning Michael Servetus for the simple reason that he voiced the idea of uniting with God (*unitarian Christians*). And even more horrible, the first Crusaders who did not hesitate to eat Arab fighters, thinking that they had no soul.[1]

In each war, each camp proclaims *"Gott mit uns"*, a motto used as a rallying cry of the Prussian army during the Thirty Years' war (*as well as on the buckle of German belts during the last World War*).

Moral principles can vary greatly from one era to the next, and also from one country to another, but with the certainty for "ordinary people" that their principles are the right ones. Many examples, even contemporary ones, could be mentioned. But as Lao Tzu points out: *"When the master makes a mistake, he realizes it. Having realized it, he admits it. Having admitted it, he corrects it."* But this realization has to occur…

So there is nothing to reproach here, except for one very important element: the binary method. The King is *"good"*, the Queen is *"good"*, this is *the order of things*. Good is this, Evil is that, because the first always triumphs according to a celestial will that is beyond the human world. Consequently, values are defined, which can only be respectable and rewarding. The notion of paradox is excluded, there is only a dichotomous approach to everything.

---

1. Amin Maalouf, *Les croisades vues par les Arabes*, J'ai lu, 1999

As soon as the child enters school, it is taught reading, writing, rhetoric and, above all, mathematics and logical-mathematical reasoning. The child's ability to analyze, reason and speculate will develop, and this will remain the only point of reference for the rest of its life *(with the exception of work on the Profound)*.

Even today, we can see that research such as the one carried out by Howard Earl Gardner[1], professor at Harvard University, is not taken into account. Research, which reveals that there are different types of intelligence.

These are currently estimated to be eight:
- verbal/linguistic intelligence
- logical/mathematical intelligence
- musical/rhythmic intelligence
- bodily/kinesthetic intelligence
- visual/spatial intelligence
- naturalistic intelligence
- interpersonal intelligence
- intrapersonal intelligence

The last one is the ability to *"access one's own feeling life — one's range of affects or emotions: the capacity instantly to effect discriminations among these feelings and, eventually, to label them, to enmesh them in symbolic codes, to draw upon them as a means of understanding and guiding one's behavior"*.

Howard Gardner also provides the following clarification:

"…a sense of self, which derives from one's peculiar blend of intelligences; an "executive capacity", which deploys specific intelligences for specific ends…"

It is this intra-personal intelligence that we are talking about…

Accordingly, the sieve used to select the specimens that are of most interest to society will be designed to target logical-mathematical intelligence, like IQ tests. And, of course, this also allows to identify the most moldable elements. Obviously, sufficient self-knowledge would be opposed to any kind of moulding *(as is the case of gifted individuals who are unable to integrate into the ambient system)*.

1. Howard Earl Gardner, *Multiple intelligences, new horizons*, Basic Books, 2006

This "moulding" can be justified, and rightly so, by *"the low evolution of our species"*, which makes it impossible to leave free will to each individual. As we have already discussed, human beings have natural impulses that are destructive (to put it mildly) and are subject to the dictates of the deep brains, their instincts and their atavism, which give free reign to the inner predator.

It is therefore essential to put in place a conditioning to curb any potential outbursts. We can only agree on the validity of this conscious or unconscious will. Free will can only be desirable when "the animal" is tamed, or better yet, killed, but this is in the realm of illusion for most people.

If in doubt, take a look around you.

The wars that punctuate our history without interruption, selfishness and egocentrism as the essential values of every human being, racism and xenophobia, whether apparent or hidden, which regularly come to the fore, latent or visible aggression whenever there is opposition, pretensions, ambient stupidity—these are only small fragments of the visible part of the iceberg of the human unconscious.

"A really negative or realistic perception?"

The answer may fluctuate, but the bottom line is that it fuels our thirst for the essential, for an escape from this stifling environment.

It is enough to see soldiers in wartime, where social morality allows one not only to break the basic laws but also to be rewarded for it (*thanks to our binary education, the paradox is not visible*). Or, as another example, we can "*extract ourselves from our human condition*" and observe from the outside our mores towards the weakest, towards the most deprived, towards animals, by reconsidering what we see as "trivial" and by refusing any cultural, religious or economic justification.

We leave you to draw your own conclusions…

Let us get back to the child's education.

The so-called pedagogical method chosen is based on imposing "truths" that are not to be discussed. The child is asked to store definitions and principles that do not vary, *dogmas, truths*. And the child will continue to do so throughout its life, victim of the imposed mould.

Could we not teach the child to nuance said values, to vary truths according to the context, to explain the paradoxical notion of Good and Evil according to the situation?

The inevitable answer will be:

"Too early for the child, let us wait for maturity!"

The only problem is, as Henri Laborit stated:

> *"I am frightened by the automatisms that can be created in a child's nervous system, without its knowledge. In adult life, it will need an exceptional luck to escape from this prison, if it ever manages to do so...[1]"*

And education, relying on affects and emotions, gives results that will not fade *(because of their impact on the Limbic)*, unless there is a deconstructive process *(affecting the Profound)*[2].

This education will continue throughout the entire early youth. The child will learn to store more or less data in drawers, to assemble and use it logically, and to discern Good from Evil according to the imposed references. And this will be true even for disciplines such as philosophy, which should, as its name suggests, be open-minded to the world, but which is nowadays limited to learning, comparing previous doctrines, and then pitting them against each other on some topic. A conditioned freedom from which the Profound is excluded.

Of course, the "quality" of this education will vary according to one's social origin.

It is obvious that if the child comes from a wealthy family, it will be moulded longer and to a greater degree, with some exceptions necessary to avoid any social disturbance. In consequence, mathematical-logical intelligence will be more developed and the child's future more optimistic. Accordingly, this type of education will create leaders who will reasonably assume that it is the only one desirable, since it was at the origin of their success.

This entire education will be effective if the reflection of the entourage

---

1. Henri Laborit, Op. cit.
2. Historically, there are extreme examples of this method of conditioning of children: the Spartans, where young people in training could practice war by murdering randomly caught slaves, the Hitler youth who fought in Berlin until Hitler's death, and today, the young fanatics of sectarian fundamentalism of all kinds.

Exaltation, emotion, deprivation, repetition — the key words of brainwashing.

is in harmony with the message instilled. No dissonance, a single message repeated day after day, without varying. What is different is an error and to be rejected. Everyone affirms it, relatives, society, media, books, politics and religion[1].

Religion, often the basis of local culture, only accentuates the initial conditioning. Religious doctrine is precise, binary, Good and Evil, rewards and punishments, theology is a science and can be taught in a rational manner. Teaching is scholastic, based on *"being as a being"*. Precise, didactic, a cold logic, without paradox, and above all, with imposed "bounds".

One may also wonder whether Western philosophy did not take the wrong path when Saint Thomas Aquinas used Aristotle's work to establish the foundation of Christian and scholastic thought with reason as a foundation *(forgetting the metaphorical dimension of Aristotle's work, such as Earth as the "center of the Universe")*.

And for those who reject any religious influence, scientific definitions and/or political doctrines substitute the missing building elements.

The structure is complete, everything is in place. Its content may change imperceptibly over time, but always by adding or removing inside each existing drawer. The references are laid, the sequence defined—*except trauma of the Profound brought on by the heart, but this is the topic of a following chapter.*

The wedding will then be celebrated in the image of a children's tales. Children will be baptized according to the ritual in place, or not, depending on one's political or family format. One will work while opposing adversarial groups *(in all Limbic logic)*, one will be manipulated by those who master this form of power, and die in fear of the unknown with the heartbreak of losing one's loved ones.

But this "portrait" would be incomplete without asking ourselves the following question:

"What is our awareness of the "self"?"

- What do we think we are?

---

[1]. For those who feel left out, either by a society that rejects them, or by a dissonant environment, the solution is to recreate a "tribe" on the margins with its own references (and impose them), or to take refuge in small groups that often bring a new, often religious, moral (requirement of the gregarious instinct), but these apparently different structures remain very defined, only the markers for Good and Evil vary.

- What do we think others think of us?

- What would we like others to think of us?

- What do others think of us?

- What would we like to be?

- What do we wish to become?

- What are we?

If we are honest with ourselves, the answers are not obvious.

We are talking, of course, about the *persona* (*in Latin "personare": speaking through*), a word that originally described the mask worn by theater actors, later taken up by C.G. Jung[1].

But it does not make sense to dissociate the persona from the deep brains; the "self" is a whole, of which the persona is only a part.

This begins in childhood. Your mom gave you a new pair of shoes (*or you stole them, according to each*). All of a sudden, while wearing them, you feel different. You have the impression that everyone is looking at you, you look at yourself in the windows, you have become different.

A child's attitude? Certainly not, because once a teenager it continues.

I find myself beautiful, ugly, small, tall, intelligent, stupid and all this represents me, I feel elevated or victim of the given image.

One might think that in adulthood maturity would make it possible to escape these chimeras, but no such luck.

Physique remains one's primary mask, and all the accessories are a second one: a beautiful car, a beautiful watch, a beautiful wedding, a social status, a house, a swimming pool, a boat, a medal, a pin. And often, appearing as even more important: the societal role, such as the profession, the function obtained. If it is rewarding, and allows to have a title, once the role has expired, how many are keen on keeping their image: "your Honor", "Master", "Doctor", "General", "Mr. Mayor", "Excellence", conflating the being and the temporary mask, confusing the illusion with the illusionist. An axiom for any societal success.

---

1. C.G. Jung, *Two essays on analytical psychology*, Collected Works, Vol. 7, Princeton University Press, 1967

"The illusion will end with the death of the illusionist", as we often say.

If one's image is less rewarding, it will influence the individual just as much. "Fortunately", one will be able to find substitutes in other groups, religious or initiatory, sport associations, unions...

Indeed, even in initiatory societies the title, the rank, are enough to make one drunk, and to avoid remaining anonymous one makes them known in a discreet, yet obvious way.

Another example is the monk's outfit, which has the advantage of blending each individual into the whole, with no difference in appearance, an objective achieved in the monastery.

But these same monks will move from one country to another, demonstrating their "perfection" by wearing their differences with robes, shaved heads or a studied look, a circumstantial smile or a grave expression, an appropriate attitude, in front of demanding audiences.

Already in his day, Kabir mocked them:

"If by shaving the head perfection is achieved, the sheep is saved, no one is lost.[1]"

And as an extreme caricature, service societies, where associations recruit only in a societal "caste" by co-optation, making it possible to differentiate oneself from the plebe and engage in self-persuasion with boastful charity events, or any other pomp and circumstance.

On the other hand, the caricatural refusal of society can also be a mask; the uniform being uniform and not uniform.

This is why Taoist and Sufi sages had no distinct appearance, blending into society (*at least originally...*). The awakened man, his ego gone, reintegrates the ordinary.

What is most astonishing is that the question of the "mask" worn no longer even arises for the ordinary person. The "self" boils down to civil status, to the illusion of the self-image. Confusion of confusions.

Obviously, education has a lot to do with this attitude. Uniforms of all kinds, whether for official or professional purposes, for social status or political rejection, are a clear reflection of the mask worn. The child dreams of a panoply and ends up identifying with it. This illusion is all-encompassing,

---

1. Yves Moatty, *Kabir: le fils de Ram et d'Allah*, Éditions Les Deux Océans, 1988

and is reflected in the child's clothing (whether for work or for vacation), physical appearance, attitude, behavior, various artifices and chosen environment.

Getting rid of it does not mean refusing the role, but rather not being fooled by it (*take a closer look at yourself and you may be surprised*).

Yet presenting oneself "naked" is part of all religious cultures. Jesus, recognizing the extent of this conditioning (*truth of yesterday and today*), said:

> "I stood at rest in the midst of the world. And unto them I was shown forth incarnate; I found them all intoxicated. And I found none of them thirsty. And my soul was pained for the children of humankind, for they are blind in their hearts and cannot see. For, empty did they enter the world, and again empty they seek to leave the world. But now they are intoxicated. When they shake off their wine then they will have a change of heart.[1]"

Of course, this does not prevent the pompous titles in most religions, even in those that advocate the non-ego: "Very Holy", "Eminence", "Monsignor", "Your Holiness", "Venerable", "Very Illustrious", etc.

What is the point of these examples?

The point is to understand the layers that cover our essential being, and which "condition" all individual perception. What we think of as our "I", our personality, is in fact only the reflection of a precise mould and the play of our deep brains. But getting rid of this hold is extremely difficult, to say the least, and the consequence of this awakening of consciousness can only be a deep-seated ill-being, as the intoxication ceases.

In conclusion of this chapter, let us follow Jesus' advice:

"Let us shake off our wine and change our hearts."

---

1. Gospel of Thomas 28

The Influence of the Subjective

In view of the preceding, at some point it becomes necessary to understand how we can be influenced by our conditioning.

Everyone thinks this is true for others, but of course not for themselves, as always...

We should ask ourselves the question: is what we see, read, hear, touch and feel at the level of the sensory real, or is it modified by an a priori, by an inculcated definition, by a learning of some kind?

Or, more directly:

"Are we victims of a societal, religious, community "brainwashing", which conditions our appreciation of everything?"

To answer this question, it is worth playing a little game. It can be used to analyze how "a point of view" can change according to a given predefinition.

First of all, it is important not to "cheat" and to be well convinced of the validity of the statements printed in bold below, **before** looking at the following images.

A silhouette is drawn below: The silhouette shows a dog with its back to you

Obvious, is it not?!

Now, another statement.

A silhouette is drawn below: The silhouette shows a dog looking at you

More or less obvious depending on the "malleability" of the brain. There are several possibilities:

- 1st possibility:

At first look at this second silhouette, I see the dog looking at me.

- 2nd possibility:

It takes me some time to "erase" the initial statement and see that the dog is looking at me.

- 3rd possibility:

I cannot see the dog looking at me. If this is the case, look at the silhouette with an intention to pull the representation toward yourself. The image should then reverse.

What information can we get out of this?

First of all, the following statement was made:

"The silhouette represents a dog."

Consequence: no questions, we recognize a dog. Yet it is only the outline of a *"shadow"*. Our brain has therefore translated this *"shadow"* into a dog *(we have no doubts)*.

Then, the second statement:

"The dog is turning its back on you."

Once this statement has been made, there are no questions about it, our first impression will be defined. We are able to see the influence that any statement, "any definition" can have on our perception.

However, there are 2 special cases not mentioned above because they are at the extremes:

Case 1:

"Despite the statement, I can only see a shadow of a dog in one direction."

This indicates a very rational mind, even too rational.

Case 2:

"Despite the statement, both directions are perceived at the same time."

This indicates a certain mental flexibility.

Most of the time, our perception stops at the provided definition. We see that the statement is indeed correct, so there is no need to go any further.

This is reassuring, because things are in their places, "we do not lose our footing".

Then the new statement:

"The silhouette represents a dog looking at you."

We look at the same silhouette again. After a more or less long adaptation period, depending on the individual, comes the mental response that enables us to discern a dog positioned in a direction opposite to the previous one.

Answer:

"Indeed, the dog is looking at me."

By repeating the exercise a number of times, it becomes possible to see the three images *(shadow = dog + two directions)* "simultaneously", without any particular mental effort.

As we discussed in a previous chapter, any definition leads to a limited or even totally conditioned perception. In other words, any given definition tends to limit the field of consciousness of a sensitive approach.

The same is true for everything, whether at the level of any one of the senses, the understanding of texts, symbols, art, etc., in one word *"EVERYTHING"*.

So, what was the point of this little demonstration?

Before answering, let us look at another example: the symbol.

Let us recall what a symbol is or should be. To avoid falling into the trap of creating a model, Carl Gustav Jung's research has been useful in finding the right approach to symbolic meaning through non-definition. A research which makes it possible to achieve an understanding of the symbol, as accurately as possible *(remember that C.G. Jung was a great lover of Orientalism, with all reserve due to his intellectualist approach to Far Eastern esotericism)*:

"What we call a symbol is a term, a name, or even a picture that may be familiar in daily life, yet that possesses specific connotations in addition to its conventional and obvious meaning. It implies something vague, unknown, or hidden from us."

"Thus a word or an image is symbolic when it implies something more than its obvious and immediate meaning. It has a wider "unconscious" aspect that is never precisely defined or fully explained. Nor can one hope to define or explain it. As the mind explores the symbol, it is led to ideas that lie beyond the grasp of reason.[1]"

The most important aspects of this non-definition are:

- *"vague, unknown, hidden, never precisely defined or fully explained, a wider "unconscious" aspect"*,

- *"beyond the grasp of our reason"*.

As with any approach, a concrete case study is necessary. Below is the "classic" representation of a Pentagram, a very ancient symbol:

And some examples of interpretations of this symbol taken at random from different *"contemporary esoteric traditions and currents"*:

---

1. C.G. Jung, *Man and his symbols*, Dell Publishing Co., 1968

- 1st example

"The connection between the superior man — the Microcosm — and the natural man must be restored. For this, a new soul has to be rebuilt.

The 5-pointed star or "Pentacle" has always been the universal symbol of this new immortal soul that can be reborn in man."

- 2nd example

"This five-pointed star symbolizes the five active principles in man: the Spirit, the Soul, the Intellect, the Heart, the Body."

- 3rd example

"The Flaming Star is our polar star, the star of free thought, an essential symbol of the rank of Companion, as can be seen in the instructions for the second symbolic rank... This rank of companion is also intimately linked to the number five: the five journeys, the five steps, the five years of age, the five lights, etc. The number five is also directly related to the Flaming Star."

- 4th example

"This is a sign of Solomon and it was used by several occult schools for spiritual improvement. A Pentagram is the symbol of the five great principles: Love, Wisdom, Truth, Justice and Virtue."

- 5th example

"A powerful and magical sign, capturing beneficial flows. The Pentagram or five-pointed star has been a sign of Health, Vitality and Positive Energy since ancient times. It has always represented light, harmony, beauty and perfection."

What can we learn from these examples?

First of all, we see a variety of interpretations for the same symbol. And, contrary to Jung's non-definition, these interpretations do not appear to be the result of a *"larger unconscious"*, but that of a *"targeted education"*.

It is obvious, however, that for the Tradition a symbol has several meanings and this helps to "open one's mind".

We could even mention our own non-definition of the symbol: "The symbol is a tool that allows, with time and the right approach, to get out of the rut of the definition thanks to the multiplicity of possible interpretations."

However, we can see that the above examples are the result of a speculative approach based on a doctrine established with reason as a support.

Following the examples cited, the question one could ask is:

"Would this kind of speculative approach lead to a greater awareness of one's Profound?"

The answer is not obvious.

Nevertheless, there is one essential condition: not to lock the recipient in a particular current of thought, corresponding to the mould "imposed" by the group or the institution. Often, this does not seem to be the case…

Let us analyze this together, knowing that we can practically always find the same strategy, whether these associations have religious, esoteric or initiatory purposes.

- Let us take as an example the path of a "layman" entering an "institution":

The "layman" enters the chosen community. His wish is obviously to be accepted, or even to rise in the hierarchy, if it exists. These two desires *(recognition and power)* are unfortunately "natural", although there are some very rare exceptions. But, as always, the individual will refuse to recognize his own motivations by telling himself: *"This is true for others but, of course, not for me."*

The community has its rules and they must be quickly understood. Additionally, it has its own culture even if it pretends to be "free". This culture will demand from the recipient to assimilate the mode of thinking to be followed, to copy the attitude of "the ideal member of the community", to reproduce the expected image and rites to be performed, to present the appropriate way of speaking.

To achieve this, the organization in question has even planned to provide the induction of answers that correspond to the stereotype of the perfect member. Documents specifying the rites and customs to be observed, the regulations to be respected, the philosophical concepts to be followed, the instructions to be learned, and possibly the hierarchical progression, are provided to avoid any unwanted or wanted interpretation. As a result, a mould is set on the appearance, progression and understanding of the symbol.

- Maybe, based on your personal experience, you think that the above description is debatable?

+ *Please verify this with an "overview".*

- *How?*

+ *If you are a member of some community, during meetings, have a look "from the outside", free of any communal "conditioning", a critical look. Or rather, should we say, an honest look. As if you were a bystander, "outside yourself", watching yourself and others act.*

As Albert Schweitzer said, "Sincerity is the foundation of spiritual life", but it should be specified: "Towards others, but also towards oneself..."

By deduction, the question that then comes to mind is:

"*Is not the best way to open this unconscious to listen to the Profound without any preconception?*"

Seems impossible? Let us *try* it as simply as possible.

First of all, observe. We can recognize in this symbol:

- *A star shape.* A learned theory or the unconscious image of a flickering star in the sky? No obvious answer here. Images seen during childhood? Something learned in school? Or an echo of the Profound?
- *With 5 points.* Infinity, unity, five elements? Which ones? Answers: our five senses, the five elements of nature, unity in the center of the creation of the five elements, another symbolism of five that I know of, etc. Intellectual, logical or intuitive deductions?
- *I "see" a man inscribed in this drawing.* Head up and the four limbs, the center is fundamental. A vision from the unconscious or a reminder of Leonardo's Vitruvius, or both?

- *etc.*

Secondly, draw the symbol and "try to live the experience". This can lead to:

- A line without beginning or end, that is, infinity—*while drawing it, for sure.*
- The beginning reaches the end, that is, unity—*effectively felt while drawing.*

And consequently:

- Does infinity meet unity and vice versa? *We get the same feeling when drawing a circle, the circle is one and infinity.*
- The pentagram is inscribed in the circle—*the difference gives birth to the identical.*
- The individual lines of the pentagram are then joined and contained within the circle, and multiplicity becomes unity. *Would this also be true for us, humans?*
- and so on.

And we see that a "relation" can be created:

- By looking at it and drawing it, I connect with this shape—*this "feeling" is important, and we will see how it relates to our topic later on.*

You can continue this work by yourself, the possibilities are endless…

We see that an approach based on our "Profound" is difficult, to say the least. How can we determine what is the product of the unconscious or the realm of our culture?

Simply looking at the symbol, it appears impossible to tell any difference. Only drawing the line, the feeling, induces some thought whose origin remains uncertain, intuitive.

So, is the experiential better connected to the Profound than the speculative? Based on our experience, this is indeed the case.

To conclude, we once again notice the significant unconscious influence that a conditioning can have on our perceptions. It remains to admit that what we think of as personal discernment is in fact only the result of a set of gobbled data—*something our ego often refuses to hear.*

Of course, when dealing with the symbol and the role of the unconscious, it seems natural that some will inquire as to its origin. C.G. Jung, through analytical psychology, explained it with a "collective unconscious[1]" shared by people regardless of place and period. This would constitute "a condition or a basis of the psyche in itself, an omnipresent, immutable condition, identical to itself in all places".

Another interesting possibility is presented by Richard Dawkins[2] — "memes". These are a kind of information transmitted from mind to mind through empathetic means. These "Memes" would have a "replicating power" similar to viruses. This means that the symbol's idea would have its own life just like other collective thoughts, and consequently behaviors.

These two theories are at the least attractive and of interest in the sense that they open a breach towards the undefined, just like a symbol does.

Both, and in particular the notion of "Memes", challenge us on what we think is the emanation of our individuality, which in this case would only be the result of an aggregate of shared, fluctuating thoughts, demonstrating that what we think of as our personality is nothing but an illusion.

Now, let us go back to our initial questioning:

"What is the point of this little demonstration?"

As we already mentioned, any perception can be heavily influenced by the different types of conditioning received, as well as by the "filters" of our deep brains. This remains equally true in all areas of the sensitive without exception *(the five senses and the "supra-sensory")*.

It is therefore necessary to take this into account in any work on the Profound and in particular when the Tools of Tradition are used.

The Tool alone is not enough. It takes a whole, a fusion between the tool and the Seeker, and to do this it is essential that the latter is in the required "state of Being". A state without preconceptions, without a priori, without any anticipation whatsoever.

It is essential not to want to define, analyze, anticipate every action, behavior, consequence, objective, otherwise the Tool will not work. This is a

---

1. *Archetypes and the Collective Unconscious (Collected Works of C.G. Jung)*, Bolingen Foundation, 1981
2. Richard Dawkins, *The Selfish Gene*, OUP Oxford, 2016

fundamental point in all authentic Traditions.

Ask yourself the following question, which echoes what we already pointed out:

> *"How to reach a veiled realm of consciousness, which cannot be comprehended because it has not been experienced, by defining beforehand an unknown sensitive perception, or else a phenomenon of indescribable transmutation?"*

Indeed, this is impossible.

The reason for that is simple. This new perception of the so-called "suprasensory" realm is inconceivable at one's current level of awareness, the "sense" in question not being awakened yet. Inconceivable because still "unreal" *(or even utopian)* for the ordinary individual. For those who prefer a more rational wording, we could say: *"The mind does not "compute"."*

So, it can be said that the Tool's purpose is to "open" one's consciousness to a new field of perception, for one to "perceive the unperceived" — *what will be left is to refine this perception.*

All authentic Traditions are about trial, the sensitive, and not Reason. This is the entire difference between the lived, "knowing", and the erudition of "knowledge".

> *"Those who know (the Tao) are not extensively learned; the extensively learned do not know it.[1]"*

That is why it is necessary to go deeper and deeper to deconstruct your conditioning by accepting its existence in the first place. Without that, how to "destroy a house" that does not exist?

> *"I will destroy this house, and none shall be able to build it again.[2]"*

Is not this deconstruction the starting point "of all great religions" that exist today?

Let us see together...

---

1. Tao Te Ching 81
2. Gospel of Thomas 71

Static and Dynamic Religion

Every Seeker looking for authenticity asks himself at some point the following question:

"Were the doctrines that support today's religions put in place by the initiators of said religious currents—Awakened Ones, Messengers, Prophets, Sons of God, Sages, whatever name history has chosen—or are they the product of a will emanating from those who succeeded them?"

The answer is important, because it underlies the direction from which to approach the dynamic[1] aspect of each religion. For, as is obvious to the initiate, the doctrines that claim to be the most enlightening or the closest to God have a hidden side, an occult current, which is not offered to the ordinary person, either in the best of cases because Tradition wants it that way, or *(quite often)* because of the loss of this dimension.

In ancient esoteric traditions, there are levels of initiation that require particular "talents", such as a broad field of consciousness and a certain quality of empathy. The obvious reasons for this are that, without the first "talent", the work elements provided would not function, and without the second, the direction the recipient might take would be towards the much more tempting dark work. It is worth pointing out that any opening of the field of consciousness modifies the "understanding" of the degrees of initiation, thanks to a perception that is more intuitive than speculative, where heart-to-heart transmission is king. Finally, it is also important to know that, according to traditional principles, we do not inform each other of the level attained by each individual.

Consequently, it is necessary to question the texts that repeat the words bequeathed by the initiators of these currents, who, it should be remembered, wrote nothing themselves.

---

1. static or dynamic religion, please refer to the introduction

Following the above and by deduction, the question that then arises is this:

"Did the heirs who retransmitted these Traditions, either orally or in writing, have the necessary degree of initiation to interpret the multiple meanings of the messages?"

It seems obvious, as any esoteric tradition demonstrates, that we cannot transmit a message requiring a certain level of initiation to someone not at this level, because the latter cannot comprehend it. Just as a metaphor cannot be interpreted out of its initiatory context, or only in a "static" manner and in the first degree — *quite common, to say the least…*

Then another question arises, just as obvious:

"Did the oral transmission suffer the clumsiness common to this type of dissemination, and the written one the possible misunderstanding of words taken out of the context of heart-to-heart communication?"

Also, it is important to remember that the formatting of these texts took place dozens or even hundreds of years after the author's "departure", with some texts reproduced identically to the original formulation, without taking into account the meaning of the popular language, the context or the complexity of the parables used — *or even with a wording modified according to the will of the powers that be.*

For example, the Bible composed of the Old Testament with the presence of a God of revenge and punishment, and the New Testament with a God of forgiveness and love.

The obvious question is:

"Why such a paradox in the same book?"

The answer of doctrinaires and exegetes is "because it has always been so" or "because Jesus was a Jew" or "because the New Testament completes and extends the Old Testament". Today, some historians suppose that it was by Constantine's will that, to make the Romans accept a religion that was too new, an ancient text was added to it.[1]"

However, reading the messages left behind, it is clear that these Messengers and Awakened Ones, seeing the limitations of their contemporaries, decided to set up the necessary safeguards for the establishment of societies

---

1. Bart Ehrman, *Lost Christianities*, Oxford University Press, 2005

on a "human" scale, in addition to an occult initiatory path intended, as always, for those *"who are worthy" (Gospel of Thomas).*

What is more, their "transcendent" awareness, and consequently the quality of their empathy, may well have produced a perception of what was desirable on the societal level, but which was unfortunately incomprehensible to ordinary people.

The origin of static religions can probably be found here: explaining an objective in the sensitive realm to those who are only at the level of the animal is obviously impossible[1].

Therefore, to reach as many people as possible, these "out of the ordinary" people have had to find parables, allegories and metaphors understandable on multiple levels: one level for ordinary people, another one for those seeking, and a last one for the most awake, namely:

- The first level is a first-degree reading or understanding of parables and allegories in accordance with the doctrine.
- The second is to be sought by oneself with the help of one's Profound, and offers indications on the path to take.
- The third gives subtle indications as to the state of being required to use the tools offered, or even the possible consequences brought about by changes in the field of consciousness; in short, the path to follow.

Today's problem, like yesterday's, the one that prompted these exceptional Beings to fight against the established religions, is that very often only the first-degree message is retained…

Let us get back to the messages inherited from around the world.

---

1. It must be said that humans, fragile beings, not very strong compared to other species, without dangerous claws or teeth, neither particularly agile nor particularly fast, without natural protection, with exposed vital organs because of the upright position, were able to survive against predators endowed with all the qualities that they did not have. Why? The answer is in our history. Humans are a real scourge, capable of killing, causing suffering, destroying everything around, including our own species, for free or for pleasure. Humans are harmful by nature and this aspect, original or consequence of the natural selection of a weak species, has certainly allowed our conservation. And we are the descendants and heirs of this scourge, our deep brains transmit to us the "qualities" required for this survival, no need to lie to ourselves.

To avoid immediate rejection, these Messengers and Awakened ones had to rely on the values, beliefs and references of their time and place to explain the inexplicable.

Unfortunately, this was often subsequently interpreted as an immutable reference.

This is an important point that has led to much confusion. Shakyamuni had to describe the path to be taken by relying on the existing foundations of Hinduism, Jesus on those of the Jews and Muhammad on those of the locals. Without this progressive approach, they would not have been heard or understood. But this "root cause", an initial constraint, is preserved today as an immutable reference.

Only the sincere Seeker accepts "the destruction of his house".

"How to know something that escapes all "common" knowledge without going through "the starting square" that is this same "common" knowledge?"

The only way to get from one bank to the other is to lean on the first to push the boat into the river between them. Then, using the boat itself will call into question the usual means of travel.

Here are some examples that have influenced contemporary society the most *(our objective is not to produce a historical or religious-philosophical comparative study, but rather a "detached" overview of each current)*:

- Buddha (Siddhartha Gautama) six centuries BC opposed the Brahmins, rejecting the very foundations of a religion that had been in place for nearly 1400 years[1].

Siddhartha's rejection applies to everything that could be considered sacred, such as: the authority of the Vedas (*reference texts*), of Brahma (*Lord of all creatures in the first degree*), cosmological theories, *Atma (theory of the self in the first degree)*, ritualism, animal sacrifices, asceticism.

Buddha's rejection of *Atma* can be seen as the rejection of a religion that is too structured, too static, based on idolatrous ritual practices. Indeed,

---

1. To the question "is Buddhism a religion?", the answer could be "yes and no". No, if we consider that the word "religion" translates as "relegere", meaning "to reread". Yes, if we interpret the same word as "religare", meaning "to connect" in the sense of "link to". Always these two aspects: static and dynamic. But today, popular Buddhism is also a static religion, with deities, deified men (including Siddhartha, the tulkus in Tantrism, etc.), prayers for gain, rigid rituals.

the notion of impermanence of the Buddhist self (*the self is like a flowing stream*) does not oppose *Atma* if we consider that the latter disappears in its union with Brahman (*the drop of water returns to the sea, or the "differentiated breath joins the undifferentiated one"*).

A revolutionary principle in the rigid society of his time, he rejected castes, asserting that *"all human beings are equal, regardless of birth, sex or race"*. Finally, he pointed out that any claim of superiority on the part of the Brahmins served only to gain economic and social advantage.

Nonetheless, to have his message accepted he had to adopt certain Hindu principles. He transformed *"metempsychosis"* into *"reincarnation"*. This *"reincarnation"* can be seen more as a *"rebirth"*, i.e. the passage from one body to another, without permanence of the "self", and not a "reincarnation" of the "self", the latter being an illusion. The notion of reincarnation can also be understood as a parable of the impermanence of the self, which is constantly changing. The "different lives" would then correspond to the eventual evolutions of one's interiority while on the initiatory path. The end of the cycles would coincide with Awakening, i.e. fusion with the One. Here, we come back to the notion of *"dying while still alive"* in initiation.

The *Sutras* of Shakyamuni's oral teaching were written several centuries after his awakening. Given the context and the words used, the historical Buddha certainly passed for an anarchist in the eyes of Hindu society at the time.

Indeed, six centuries later, Jesus *(Yehoshua: God saves)* followed the same path, with a strikingly similar approach. Born into Jewish society, Jesus acted like a revolutionary. He distanced himself from the Torah, also questioning the ritual if it did not testify to a sincere desire to purify the heart, just like "*The Sabbath was made for man, and not man for the Sabbath*" (Mark 2:27), and "*But <only> the true circumcision in the spirit gives all profit!*" (Thomas 53). He overturned the tables of the merchants in the temple of Jerusalem, whom he called "*thieves*", (*which can also be an allegory about the inner fight to be waged*), also refused the asceticism of John the Baptist; he was even "*a glutton and a drunkard*" for his enemies (Matthew 11:19), banished revenge "*But I tell you, love your enemies…*" (Matthew 5:44). He declared himself the "*Son of God*", blasphemy par excellence for Jewish society at the time.

However, he kept the notion of a single God and "Father" *(an anthropomorphism understandable by all)*. He also preserved the notion of paradise and hell *("Sheol" and "Abraham's bosom" in Judaism)*, which, same as with Buddhist *"reincarnation"*, can be understood as a parable of the mystic's rebirth after having had a *"union" (connecting)* with the Absolute, with God. This may correspond to "Paradise". "Hell", on the other hand, may be the allegory of the opening of consciousness to the dark work, as we shall see later. Without wanting to offend anyone's convictions, the resurrection of Christ *("anointed by God")* following his crucifixion may also signify that his message is still alive in his disciples, past and present.

Similarly to Siddhartha Gautama *(Buddha)*, his words are humanistic in essence, offering *"forgiveness"*, *"love for one's neighbor"*, up to self-sacrifice.

He offers an initiatory Path that leads to a deconstruction of the "self", a consequence of "hollowing work"[1], in total opposition to the exoteric doctrine in place.

Some of Jesus' sayings may be confusing, but he is indeed speaking about the inner struggle, the deconstruction of the "self", of the "persona", in order to reach the essence:

"I will destroy this house, and none shall be able to build it again.[2]"

"Think not that I am come to send peace on earth: I came not to send peace, but a sword.[3]"

"Do you think I came to bring peace on earth? No, I tell you, but division.[4]"

As with Buddha, the basics remain the same: do not kill, do not steal, in short, do not harm your fellow man.

Following Buddha (523 BC), Lao Tzu and Confucius (all born in the 6th century BC), Muhammad was born in Mecca in the 6th century AD. Like Siddhartha and Jesus, he had to face opposition from the people of his birthplace, as "no one is a prophet in their own land".

---

1. Work of dismantlement (of the ego, individuation, persona) and not to bring new knowledge.
2. Gospel of Thomas 71
3. Matthew 10:34
4. Luke 12:51

According to Islamic tradition, as a "Messenger" he brought the word of God communicated to him by Archangel Gabriel, and publicly declared that *"God is One"*.

As with Christianity, the first converts were persecuted and murdered, when Muhammad clashed with the often idolatrous beliefs of the local tribes. The ban on representing God in this tradition is certainly a consequence of the rejection of idolatry of any "image", but above all, this "non-representation" can be compared to a symbolic abstraction.

The Quran *(collection of divine messages transmitted by Muhammad)*, the Sunnah *(the record of Muhammad's words and deeds)*[1], same as the Gospels, would have been compiled by his disciples after his death.

He is considered as the successor of the different Prophets of the Book, Adam, Noah, Abraham, Moses, Jesus. He kept the Kaaba pilgrimage. He communicated strict rules of life, making it possible to establish a stable society, but also a religious message whose approach and interpretations vary according to the different currents that followed his death, as was the case for Buddhism and Christianity.

We can see that the evolution of any religion is characterized by a dilution of its essence over time.

The Awakened ones, or Messengers of God, whatever we call them, opposed the existing institutions that represented the local religions, not because they were empty of any spiritual path, but because the understanding of it had disappeared.

It is likely that the governing structures of these religions, because of their rigidity, no longer allowed for a sensitive, intuitive understanding of the message left behind, the static dimension becoming the only possible interpretation of the reference texts and oral traditions. Confusion par excellence.

But it is fair to say that, given people's low level of evolution, the initiatory messages of Shakyamuni, Jesus and Muhammad were quickly covered, at least in part, by the same mantle. The exoteric dimension of the reference

---

1. "Muhammad's companions had memorized the Quran while the Prophet was proclaiming it under divine inspiration. There were also elements written on makeshift materials. All of these were "collected" to be united in the Quran." (Alfred Louis de Prémare, *Les collections de l'Histoire*, 2006)

texts no doubt reflects this constraint. Muhammad applied it forcefully, in a context of constant conflict.

The "heirs" of Buddha and Jesus, for their part, in a less tormented but not more ideal environment, chose a second solution[1], which consisted in applying a new conditioning to Man, that is, imprinting a message at the level of the unconscious *(Limbic brain)* by means that so-called initiatory or esoteric circles often use unknowingly *(we clearly specify "new conditioning" and not "initiation")*.

Accordingly, differentiating between the two aspects of religion should be done not through a syncretism of bookish theories, but on the basis of shared experiences of real-life initiations.

Let us begin with the static dimension:

To understand this dimension, we have to look at the ordinary person. He apprehends everything through his reason, which can be more or less developed. He is both dependent on it and on his deepest nature, as we discussed earlier. As a result, even when his analytical logic shows him that an action is justified, he is still dependent on this nature, this instinct, which is under the control of his deep brains *(which are insensitive to logic)*. However, the conditioning imposed during his childhood can force him to play the desirable social role of the surrounding environment, of the group.

The conditioning consists of:

- influencing through abstinence: fasting *(hunger or thirst break down "barriers")* and sex *(abstinence before marriage promotes the submission of adolescents, followed by the obvious "reward")*.

- influencing the emotional dimension through common rituals based on the emanation of an egregore *("emotional entity")* as a result of a combination of factors such as ceremonial aspect, subliminal evocation, rhythm, sound, drama or joy. In other cases, by a more immediate action on fear, amazement or emotional shock.

---

1. Pierre Riffard, *Ésoterisme d'ailleurs*, Éditions Robert Laffont, 1997: "We are talking about the structures put in place following their departure. In reality, Siddhartha lived like his monks, begging with a bowl, and Jesus preached under constant threat from religious and military authorities. The story goes that Buddha converted a king, monks and nuns, as well as lay people. He had to "resign himself" (?) to issuing rules: 253 for monks and 440 for nuns, just as Muhammad had to do orally for his disciples."

- influencing the gregarious dimension of the human species: desire to be "recognized", threats of rejection, exclusion; not to be loved anymore.
- influencing the deep desire for security: threats of immediate repercussions *(boomerang effect, divine punishment, karma)*.
- influencing self-esteem: to be recognized, to be loved by the group.
- influencing the sexual dimension: control of the union, prohibitions, to be the reference for the other sex *(reincarnation into a superior man, "idol", saint, pack leader)*.

Secondly, as with any species:

- punishment: metempsychosis *(in inferior species)*, reincarnation *(in an inferior man)*, rejection, and hell.
- reward: end of all suffering, reincarnation into a superior "being", medals, paradise.

Without forgetting the obligatory tireless repetition: the same message repeated endlessly to better imprint it in the Limbic brain (long memory). And to arouse interest, bring in the wonderful, the prodigious, wave the "rattle".

It should be stressed that, in order to avoid pitting the Neocortex against the Limbic brain, reason against the imposed mould, it is necessary to provide a logical and rational explanation in parallel. However, let us not forget that trying to explain the inexplicable is impossible, and trying to make it understood is a wasted effort. What is more, approaching the incomprehensible by making ordinary people "lose their reason" could only lead to extremes that would be, to say the least, unfortunate for society.

Imagine the ordinary person being told *(to paraphrase Buddhism in part)*:

"You are just an illusion, a drop of water that tomorrow will join the sea, losing all awareness of your individuality. No threat awaits you, you are free to do whatever you want or think, you will not be and cannot be punished."

We dare not think what our humanity would be with religious foundations like these.

So, everything is defined precisely, compared with examples from other currents *(always the notion of Good and Evil from the "binary" logic of the intellect)*, and a "science of religions" is set up, a theology mastered by the Knowedgeables.

Contours and colors are determined, one remains in the figurative, even for divine or enlightened notions. This is the role of religious scholastic education. Discursive analysis is king, so no one risks drowning in the unknown. A hierarchical structure is put in place, in harmony with that of society and reassuring it. Not to mention the anthropomorphic dimension of God, which enables reason to "keep its footing", or otherwise deify the Awakened.

This is also the case for Buddhist doctrine, Buddha's pictorial story and the deities, which define an exoteric dimension that enables us to draw an analogy with monotheism.

It should be noted that the first two purely esoteric schools of Buddhism (Primitive Buddhism and Dhyana) were created during Buddha's lifetime. The Lesser and Greater Vehicle, exoteric or mesoteric schools, depending on one's analysis, were established after his death.

And one last point. History clearly shows that, "victims" of their predatory instinct, as soon as the threat disappears, people are inclined to commit all kinds of excesses. Theft, rape and murder are the lot of any war. Like unruly children, people need a threatening authority to respect morality. Once the father's authority has disappeared, on the societal level, the law and its representatives are there to replace it.

For monotheistic religions, reinforcing this threat is God's vigilance, presented as that of a caring Father who can bring, according to a defined morality, the deserved punishment or reward. The symbol of the Father is effective because it acts on the unconscious *(except, of course, when the anchored memory is linked to neuroses)*. This Father is a man of a dimension beyond reason, his potentialities exceeding human understanding.

In popular Buddhist movements, Shakyamuni is deified and presented as omnipresent and omniscient. Moreover, in accordance with the society of the time: Buddha is the son of a reigning prince and Jesus a descendant of David *(an exoteric dimension that is accepted by the Limbic, in phase with societal conditioning and bound to be accepted by the powers that be)*.

This has qualities and defects, advantages and disadvantages.

The obvious qualities are:

- accepting that our senses cannot perceive everything,
- understanding that our intellect cannot comprehend everything,
- accepting "submission to a supra-human order".

However, the actual consequences are negative, to say the least. Indeed, God *(or divinity)* is seen as an "external" anthropomorphized being endowed with powers, therefore:

- He is and will remain "external", inducing a total separation between man and God.
- His reasoning is binary, like that of a human, causing crises of Faith *(or should we say belief)* when the ordinary person judges that divine decisions are not in accordance with morality *(or the "logic" of his Karma)*.
- to have His favor it is enough to respect the teaching of the authorities, to observe the precepts and to practice the rituals.

The path is discipline, submission, and above all dogmatism, governed by a "religious elite" holding all authority.

To escape this static dimension, some take refuge in a different teaching, thinking that the origin of this sclerosis comes from the initial message or the existing structure[1].

We can cite the conversion of many Christians to Tibetan Buddhism as an example for the West. Yet, just like Christianity, Buddhism has its own canons, definitions, doctrines, deities, rites and processions. We find again, although in a different version, the threat of the afterlife necessary to the establishment of desirable morality, the marvelous aspect of the chosen one, a highly organized and hierarchical institution stemming from the feudal system that saw their birth. Saints are replaced by Tulkus *(accredited by religious authorities and worshipped in the same way by devotees)*, the Pope by the Dalai Lama *(temporal and religious power, "Most Holy Father" on the one hand, "His Holiness" on the other)*, Jesus by Buddha *("divine" dimension or wonderful predestination)*.

---

1. In his study of the different types of intelligence, Howard Gardner points out that a lack of self-knowledge (intrapersonal intelligence) leads to looking for an external culprit for one's own failures.

Everything is exactly the same, only the wrapping has changed.

In both cases:

- *Messenger and Awakened have extraordinary abilities (reality or parable?). Jesus and Buddha walk on the water, know the thoughts of others, perform wonders.*
- *Messenger and Awakened are predestined; Buddha presents 32 main signs and 80 secondary signs[1] of the Great Man; for Jesus, it is the announcement of the Angel.*
- *Messenger and Awakened are both, according to the texts, born of a virgin.*

Metaphors taken in the first degree? Or static dimension?

Let us remove the packaging and try to outline what some call "*the contradiction between the notion of God and that of Awakening*", by immersing ourselves beforehand in the expression of the Prior of Mont des Cats Abbey:

"*To want to define God is to distance oneself from Him!*"

Of course, we realize that this is impossible; non-definition is the common property of both notions and the contradiction voiced, in this case, is the expression of the limit of the one expressing it.

The apocryphal Gospel of Thomas, too, erases any desire for differentiation, particularly in the following saying, which does away with any opposition between Buddhist "awakening" and the "union" described by Jesus:

"*I am the all; the all came forth from me, and the all attained to me. Cleave a (piece of) wood; I am there. Raise up a stone, and you will find me there.[2]*"

And that the "self" is an illusion:

"*Be passersby.[3]*"

As "the drunkenness" described in this gospel shows, the rigid doctrine of each religion often makes practitioners blind and deaf.

Presumably, everything we have just said about "static religion" must have corresponded to the state of existing religions when Shakyamuni, Jesus and

---

1. Louis Renou, Jean Filliozat, *L'inde classique. Manuel des études indiennes*, A. Maisonneuve, 1991
2. Gospel of Thomas 77
3. Gospel of Thomas 42

Muhammad took action to awaken dormant spirituality in their lands.

But it is in the nature of ordinary people to repeat the same mistakes. From a geopolitical point of view, this is self-evident, and it can be feared that very quickly, following the departure of their initiators, the religions mentioned followed the same path.

But, we repeat, there is no criticism in what we say. It was, and still is, essential that a basic moral be imposed on the ordinary person, and we can only thank these enlightened people for the message they left us.

The basis of the common message is the one summarized by Confucius six centuries BC:

"All men between the four seas are brothers."

"Do not do unto others what you would not like to be done to you.[1]"

Those at the origin of the religions mentioned had to reject the existing static approach, but above all their spiritual qualities allowed them to regain their lost essence.

It is up to each person to discover the hidden meaning of the messages left, and to seek the proper use of the tools bequeathed since the dawn of time. Then, all that remains is to follow the Seeker's discreet path.

And to do this, let us ask ourselves the question: *what characterizes dynamic religion?*

First of all, it would be interesting to know precisely and in detail what has been hidden in the history of the three religions mentioned, namely:

- the 5 years *(or 7, depending on the sources)* of Buddha's asceticism.
- the probable stay of Jesus with the Essenes, renowned for their asceticism, before his 30th birthday.
- the long period when Muhammad regularly retired to the caves of Mount Hira to meditate before his 40th birthday.

This would suggest that their Revelation or Awakening was the result, in addition to "extraordinary" personal qualities, of work on the Profound (*i.e. "connecting"*).

---

1. Henri Borel, op. cit.

Buddha's rejection of asceticism is not at odds with our assertion that *"once the door has been opened, it can no longer be closed"*, and that we must then know how to become "natural" again, to put ourselves back into the "uniform" of a person of ordinary appearance.

Indeed, it can be said that without total personal involvement, no religion could be dynamic. One cannot exist without the other, and vice versa.

But let us first specify what dynamic religion is not, namely the "superficial work" that is found in all static religions or exoteric teachings. "Superficial work" consists in accumulating the greatest amount of knowledge about a chosen teaching and then reproducing it conceptually.

For example:

- learning all the writings, the collected words, as well as their "official" interpretations.

- seeking out the lesser-known anecdotes, thinking that they contain hidden knowledge, magic formulas, believing that they work by themselves *(abracadabra!)*, in short, a "magical" realm where personal effort is excluded.

- learning the history, dates of each event, places, geopolitical context.

- analyzing all the theories developed by the doctrine, without questioning a single one of them. They become one's own, as if obtained by a revelation. They are absolute truth.

- adorning oneself with the attire corresponding to the stereotyped image, aping the ideal attitude, codified gestures, chosen words. All to reproduce the perfect "image" *(a new mask)*.

- reciting prayers, verses, mantras, like a "parrot", without changing state, to gain, to be heard, to listen to oneself. To act as if...

- respecting the established structure, without observing its qualities.

- submitting to human authority in the spiritual realm.

- admiring the magnificence of the rituals and contributing to them.

- wanting to be a cog inside the whole, so becoming one.

- representing the teaching, or creating a tributary.

In short, this does not differ in any way from the construction of a societal mould and does not influence the Profound. Whether one practices for a year, ten years, fifty years, no metamorphosis will be possible, nothing will change at the level of one's field of consciousness, stereotypes rule. The religion is said to be static.

This is of course in opposition to the "hollowing work" of the dynamic or esoteric religion[1], which can be described in this way:

- not neglecting knowledge, but placing it where it should be—in the cultural realm.
- reading the writings, the various commentaries, but while opening one's intuition to all possible interpretations, one's own, those of opposite teachings, those obtained "who knows how".
- theories are seen as possibilities, but without being burdened by them when working with the tools that allow Realization.
- realizing that appearances are a mistake, that playing a role is a distraction that confuses being with appearance.
- not playing with appearance or attitude, interiority rules.
- merging, forgetting oneself in the tools provided, like a shelter that opens out into the infinite, like a bottomless pit.
- taking as one's referents those who can show the right way to use the tools, and not the official structure, in complete confidence.
- rituals performed in common are shunned because they represent the superficial.
- withdrawing from any structured whole; any formalization is alienating and actually opposes the path to be followed.
- belonging to nothing, or rather to the Whole.
- deferring to the indefinite, the infinite, the intangible, the Absolute. Experience is the only beacon.

The sensitive state varies, evolves day to day, making that of the moment quite mediocre compared to that of the next day, and the result is humility.

---

1. By esoteric we do not mean a hidden doctrine, but the character of that which is impenetrable to the "ordinary person".

The whole is dynamic.

"Nice list", you might say, *"but what about the existing religions in all this?*

If we take into consideration the motivation of the initiators of the religions mentioned, it seems obvious that they possess all the tools required to make them dynamic, that is why they exist.

Some tools, however, are hidden, or even lost.

Let us continue on our path.

Esoteric Texts

The fact is that all religions have two sides, one intended for the ordinary person, responsible for providing the necessary morality for the establishment of a society with a "human" dimension, the other initiatory, intended for those able *(or destined)* to follow this path. The great difficulty for the Seeker is to discern *the wheat from the chaff*, and it can be feared that, without an initial knowledge of an ancestral initiatory Tradition, this will prove particularly challenging.

As previously discussed, most of the commentaries provided on the texts available to the general public are made by Knowledgeables who delight in developing theories inside the chosen doctrines. This is, of course, the role of religious structures and scholars from any country.

However, when one has the privilege of being the heir to an authentic tradition of whatever origin, one can easily realize that there is a diluted trace of the original spiritual essence in each religion.

This may offend some readers, however all those who have been introduced to a true "primordial tradition", of any country, recognize each other and speak the "same language". The reason for that is that only the packaging changes, the common essence of the "universal primordial tradition[1]" requires taking similar paths.

Moreover, it seems obvious, by consulting the various available documents, that some manuscripts have been written with the main objective of preserving the esoteric tradition of their movement. And we can also assume that many have been destroyed or lost.

---

1. Primordial tradition: meaning the one transmitted since the dawn of time, universal by the nature of man.

To bring out the common essence of the messages left, we have chosen certain passages from four texts from different religions, different periods, and different locations, separated by thousands of kilometers.

First of all, the Gospel of Thomas, a manuscript in Coptic language that was discovered in Upper Egypt by peasants in 1945. It is an apocryphal gospel known to theologians, whose trace had been lost since the fourth century. It should be noted that it was during this period that the list of canonical writings was imposed by the powerful Pope of Alexandria Athanasius (in 367), just as the reading of texts not on the list was forbidden. As Bart Ehrman writes, it is likely that the monks of the Pachomian monastery, trying to save the forbidden manuscripts from destruction, lost them in the nearby desert[1].

As a reminder, the primitive title of this gospel was:

"These are the hidden words that the living Jesus spoke. And Didymos Judas Thomas wrote them down.[2]"

(Didymos in Greek is the twin or rather "the one who has the same accomplishment")

He recounts the esoteric teaching of Jesus:

"... And he took him, withdrew, and said three sayings to him. Now, when Thomas came to his companions they asked him, "What did Jesus say to you?", Thomas said to them, "If I say to you one of the sayings that he said to me, you will take stones and stone me, and fire will come out of the stones and burn you up.[3]"

Anecdote and/or parable also used by Matthew, Mark and Luke. The Gospel of Thomas therefore corresponds to the hidden part of Christianity. This is echoed in the following sayings:

"I speak my mysteries to those [who are worthy of my] mysteries. What your right hand does, let not your left hand know what it does.[4]"

---

1. Bart Ehrman, *Lost Christianities*, Oxford University Press, 2005
2. Metanoïa, *Gospel according to Thomas*, Éditions Dervy, 1990
3. Gospel of Thomas 13
4. Gospel of Thomas 62

> "Do not give dogs what is holy, and do not throw your pearls before pigs, lest they trample them underfoot and turn to attack you.[1]"

The following could be, in the eyes of those who have had an experience of the Profound, a proof, if proof were needed:

> "I am the all; the all came forth from me, and the all attained to me.[2]"

Which, far from being a parable, corresponds to the lived experience of the Union.

The established religious institution is criticized not only for having hidden the keys to knowledge, but also for failing to use them.

> "... The Pharisees and the scribes have taken the keys of knowledge (and) have hidden them. They did not go in, and those who wished to go in they did not allow.[3]"

The most astonishing aspect of this manuscript is its predictive power:

> "The stone the builders rejected has become the cornerstone...[4]"

Clearly, as this Gospel demonstrates, those who belonged to this current of Christianity were familiar with the tools of the Profound. This is why the Gospel of Thomas allows an intuitive approach, offering images that call out to the Profound; provided, of course, that one's own conditioning does not obscure it too much.

And while quoting esoteric texts we should also mention original Taoism.

First of all, it is worth pointing out that Taoism today has become, in most cases, a confused system of magic, alchemy and idolatry that has nothing to do with the mystical teaching at its origin. Today's so-called "religious" rituals are more in the realm of superstition and belief in the negative sense of the terms, something we will not go into here.

An "amusing" example in Taoist temples is a statue of a horse which is supposed to heal you when you rub the spot corresponding to the area affected by an ailment with your hand (amusing, but reminiscent of other "local" examples).

---

1. Matthew 7:6
2. Gospel of Thomas 77
3. Gospel of Thomas 39
4. Psalm 118:22

Speaking of excesses, we will avoid mentioning Westerners who dress up in carnival costumes to imitate the old Taoist Masters, as this would be an incursion into the "Land of Absurdity".

Indeed, this is also the case with Taoism *(with Lao Tzu (513 BC), then Lieh-Tzu (399 BC) and Chuang Tzu (320 BC))* whose texts, abstract to say the least, and with multiple levels of understanding, were transposed into a doctrine two centuries later, with links to a multitude of concepts such as the five elements *(earth, water, fire, wood, metal)* and their interactions, as well as the dualism of Yin and Yang, which is not really a dualism at all, and which merely throws another obstacle on the path of the Seeker. Not to mention the *I Ching (Yijing)*, originally presenting a certain "simplicity" resulting from observation of nature, understandable only by "realized people", which grew in complexity in three stages *(3000, 1122, 1000 BC)*, and was then interpreted by Confucian scholars in the 4th century BC[1].

But let us go back to original Taoism, not concerned with society. This path to realization has but one objective: accomplishment of the individual.

It should be noted that the Tao is not only the "Way", as it is too often described, but also the *"indefinable"*, the *"inexpressible"*, the *"nameless" (wu ming)*, the *"imageless" (wu xiang)*, a notion of an *"absolute"* that cannot be apprehended by pure Reason, but only through experience.

Not a "God" as an external entity, but an *"All"* with which we can enter into harmony, union *(connection)*, even fusion, reminiscent of the "God" of Sufism *(introduced into China in 905, has it, more or less, undergone Chinese influence?)* or the "God" of the apocryphal Gospel of Thomas, and even more elusive, comparable to "an infinite symbolic abstraction".

> *"There was something undefined and complete, coming into existence before Heaven and Earth. How still it was and formless, standing alone, and undergoing no change, reaching everywhere and in no danger (of being exhausted)! It may be regarded as the Mother of all things.[2]"*

---

1. Dates according to the chronology given by Pierre Rifard in *Ésotérisme d'ailleurs*, Éditions Robert Laffond, 1997
2. Tao Te Ching 25

This reminds Sikhism:

"God is infinite, eternal, without form or attributes, unknowable, ineffable and omnipresent [1]..."

Just like Gnostic Christianity:

"Thomas said to him: Master, my mouth is wholly incapable of saying whom you are like.[2]"

The anthropomorphic notion is totally proscribed, no logic can define the Tao, but on the contrary, we can, like water flowing freely around a rock, following the slope, naturally act in harmony with the Tao *(Wu Wei)*.

But this "naturalness" is the result of a transformation, or rather, a "rediscovery" of one's original state.

Lao Tzu specifies:

"I alone seem listless and still, my desires having as yet given no indication of their presence. I am like an infant which has not yet smiled. I look dejected and forlorn, as if I had no home to go to.[3]"

Any approach based on Reason or discursive analysis is impossible, only experience counts.

Chuang Tzu (Zhuangzi) evokes this principle in the following wish:

"Where can I find a man who has forgotten words so I can have a word with him?[4]"

Is this the same as the "I can neither read nor write" in Hui Neng, Kabir and Muhammad?

Lao Tzu affirms it:

"Words that are strictly true seem to be paradoxical.[5]"

To achieve this experience, you need to "knock on the Dark Barrier" and have a Master willing to teach you a whole range of methods aimed at merging with the Tao, becoming aware of the "All".

---

1. Denis Matringe, Excerpt from the article *"L'Âdi Granth et Guru Nânak"*, Le Point Références, March-April 2012
2. Gospel of Thomas 13
3. Tao Te Ching 20
4. *The Complete Works of Zhuangzi*, Columbia University Press, 2013
5. Tao Te Ching 78

Classically, this usually translates into: Refining the "vitality" into breath *(the Jing into Chi)*, refining the breath into Spirit *(the Chi into Shen; "Shen, Celestial Spirit" in opposition to "Gui, terrestrial spirit")*, refining the Spirit into "opening" *(the internal breath joining the external one, "the Spirit breaks the crust")* to "merge with the Tao", the microcosm joining the macrocosm.

The objective, which is in fact a "non-objective", because any willpower is to be proscribed, can be achieved thanks to the "internal work" *(Nei Kung, or Neigong)* described. It is a spiritual Realization, which transforms the individual by altering his field of consciousness.

This is not to be confused with contemporary *"Chi Kung" (Qigong)*, which is a by-product of this spiritual path. In the latter, the work to be carried out is based on Reason or pseudo-knowledge of the phenomenon sought, with the willed objective of physical and mental well-being *(this is the exoteric approach, the first degree)*.

And we should also mention the Taoist "Immortals" *(Zhenren: "True/Genuine Person")* and related "Internal Alchemy" *(Neidan)*. Numerous legends and popular beliefs have sprung from this metaphor, which evokes the "supreme initiation" attained by a few Awakened Ones.

Just as Arab and Western alchemy saw the "object" *(transmutation of metal)* become more important than the Realization itself, so China saw the "object" *(the body)* of its alchemy become the essence of the quest, forgetting that the exoteric dimension could only oppose the "right" state of the Seeker. This was so widespread that some Chinese emperors even organized official expeditions to seek out these famous immortals of legend, and established public cults to attract them.

The primary text of reference in Taoism is the *Tao Te Ching*. The most accurate translation of the title according to us is "Classic of the Way and its virtue". This work was left by Lao Tzu to the guardian of the Western Pass, when the old sage decided to disappear without a trace — the famous representation of this Master, riding a buffalo, determined "to enter the Mystery". Legend or reality, the metaphor corresponds well to the book's philosophy. Abstraction is the rule, and intuition alone must lead the way, obliterating anything superfluous. The numerous translations and interpretations vary the meaning of this text considerably, even bringing about significant contradictions. As always, and as this Classic points out, experience is the only way to understand certain passages, not through reasoning, but by resonating with the Profound.

As always, it has to be reminded that *"Traduttore, traditore" (to translate is to betray)*, which is true at the level of classical literary Chinese translated to Western languages, but also in China itself where ancient manuscripts seem to partly contradict today's texts. Moreover, who can understand perfectly the meaning of the words, expressions and metaphors of the original text, intended for a restricted group of initiates *(which is still the case for any esoteric text)*, 2500 years later? Customs and culture have changed, to say the least. That is why, throughout this book, we have chosen to extract only that which really "resonates", that which speaks to the Profound and remains unchanging.

Original Taoism presents itself as a Path of transcendence, and Lao Tzu's image is that of an experienced man who lived it and is totally imbued with it. The many possible interpretations mean that, throughout his Quest, the Seeker can see a reflection of the path he has taken.

Of course, when speaking of Taoism, one also necessarily invokes Buddhism. Historically, these two movements have strongly influenced each other in China. What is more, the old Taoist Masters said that Buddhism was similar to original Taoism.

It should be remembered that Chan was introduced into China in 520 AD by Bodhidharma, the 18th Dhyana Patriarch, who thus became the 1st Patriarch of this Chinese movement. Chan is the spiritual school that has left the greatest mark on ancient Chinese tradition. The reason for this strong imprint is due to the personality of Bodhidharma, who was, according to legend, the creator of the martial arts of the famous Shaolin temple.[1]

Chan *(which gave rise to Zen in Japan, with Japanese rigor as a complement)* means "meditation"; but at this point we must correct a rather common mistake. Meditation does not mean *"to subject oneself to a long reflection"*, i.e. to examine an idea in greater depth, as our dictionaries specify. It

---

[1]. Shaolin was the center of Buddhist martial arts, while Mount Wudang was the center of Taoist arts. Shaolin has today been recreated from scratch *(including humans)* for tourist purposes by the Chinese government, preserving the myth of its origin.

comes from meditari, which means *"to be led to the center*[1]*"*, and Chan can only be approached through this meaning. Here too, modern people would translate this as their own center *(egocentrism be damned!)*. But it has to be understood as the center of everything, which, paradoxically, is everywhere.

Chan therefore corresponds to the Indian Dhyana, whose origins date back to the 5th century BC. Its main aim is to liberate us from illusory dualistic thinking. The basic "method" is meditation, with the idea of "letting go", the rest is theory. The "letting go" is the absence of will, of action at the level of the "voluntary system", which keeps the mind struggling with the current of thoughts that has to dry up. Once thoughts subside, the mind must escape the prison of the ego, the illusion of the "Self", to finally awaken, i.e. break the subjective barrier between individuality and the "All", the "One".

"One is All, All is one" Seng Ts'an

We allow ourselves to make a parenthesis on the well-known Zen principle of living in the "present moment". This illusory dream, given to even the most informed layman, could lead one to believe that attention alone, or concentration, would be enough to awaken.

If that was the case, the attentive viewer, the pool player, would have the "right state" for the Path. Just as in Taoism, the "breath" is the link which, over time, makes it possible to "be led". Also, the right movement is made not with concentration or attention *(the first stage)*, but through rediscovered naturalness, through connection with the "One", through the communion, and in rare cases, through the fusion which cannot be achieved when one's "own presence" is still too strong.

So where does the difference lie between Taoism and Buddhism? Nowhere *(just like for primitive Christianity, Sufism, hermeticism, and all primordial traditions)*. Only the method varies and only superficially. It is possible to say that Taoism allows to work on the body in order to reach the Spirit, while Buddhism abstracts the body in order to find the Spirit. However, these quests are full of paradox, where no truth exists, no affirmation can therefore be given, no definition can see the light of day, only one's subjective experience can be the answer.

---

1. Karlfied Graf Durckheim, Courrier du Livre

The historical text of Chan is the *Hsin Hsin Ming (Verses on the Faith-Mind)* by Seng Ts'an, 3rd Patriarch of Chan. It is exemplary as a working guide. Legend has it that Seng Ts'an was a leper when he met the 2nd Patriarch Hui Neng. Hui Neng had his awakening with Bodhidharma after asking him to set to rest his troubled mind. The answer he received was *"bring me your mind and I will set it to rest"*; with Hui Neng unable to bring it, Bodhidharma told him *"You see, I have already set it to rest"*, thus causing the Awakening. As for Seng Ts'an, his Awakening was similar.

Beautiful stories, right? However, they can be seen as carrying the principles to be respected during meditation, which can be condensed to *"attaining a state located outside any intellectual conception"*, i.e. seeing things as they are.

This is the state of the newborn *(or early childhood)*, which consists in *"being naked"*, according to Christian tradition.

Let us ask ourselves the following questions:

"What differentiates God from Tao, from the All?"

"The Awakening from fusion with the Tao, from union with God?"

The following answer may come to mind:

"Nothing, except probably our own limits and illusions".

But this apparent simplicity, this ease of access, can only be achieved by our confused and complicated mind after a long journey through the meanders of the paradox.

"No matter how things are conditioned, whether with 'to be' or 'not to be',

It is manifest everywhere before you.

The infinitely small is as large as large can be,

When external conditions are forgotten;

The infinitely large is as small as small can be,

When objective limits are put out of sight.[1]"

These lines represent the essence of Chan teaching, a school of "immediateness".

"When all things are seen equally, the timeless Self-essence is reached.

---

1. Ibidem

No comparisons or analogies are possible in this causeless, relationless state.¹"

As we are quoting esoteric texts, we should also mention someone who revolted in the 15th century against the impoverishment of the established religions. Like Shakyamuni, Jesus and Muhammad, he rebelled against the formalism of the structures charged with transmitting the message of the various religious currents, against the rigid doctrines, the intellectualism of the Knowledgeables, the limitations of the ordinary person.

"If you see the One, you have the Gnosis, Otherwise your science is only ignorance!²"

He advocated a sensitive approach outside any discursive logic, eliminating all dualism.

"When I was, Hari [God] was not, and now Hari is and I am no more: All darkness vanished, when I saw the Lamp within my heart.³"

Like Shakyamuni, Jesus, and Muhammad, he did not write anything and his words, represented in several thousand poems, are at the origin of an oral tradition that was, in part, transcribed by disciples in various books.

He expressed, without any concessions, all the discrepancies that exist between the original message and the one expressed by the established institutions.

"The parrot gabbles "God" like a man but doesn't know God's glory.⁴"

He indicated the path to be followed with clarity, eliminating any ostentatious devotion, obvious proof of transcendent knowledge. Just as for Jesus, the "destruction of the house" is the hollowing work to be undertaken.

"A violent fire caught in the wooden house: The Pandit full of science is only a pile of ashes, but luckily the ignorant has been preserved!⁵"

Like Shakyamuni, he opposed castes, nationalism, advocating that people are equal.

"I and you are of one blood, and one life animates us both; from one mother

---

1. Ibidem
2. Yves Moatty, *Kabir: le fils de Ram et d'Allah*
3. Kabir, *"Kabir" Volume One*, Charlotte Vaudeville, Oxford University Press
4. *The Bijak of Kabir*, translated by Linda Hess and Shukdeo Singh
5. Yves Moatty, *Kabir: le fils de Ram et d'Allah*

is the world born; what knowledge is this which makes us separate?"

A humble weaver in Benares, his words, whose simplicity can only illuminate the path of every Seeker, are revered by Hindus, Muslims and Sikhs alike. It is a teaching that has nothing to envy of the traditions of the Far East.

"In the heart of the truth-loving person is the dwelling place of God.[1]"

Like Muhammad and Hui Neng, he could neither read nor write. The name of this extraordinary man was Kabir.

Here we will pause for a moment to mention the relation with the "object[2]". We will come back to this "work" in more detail later. Its "nature" is strikingly recalled *(for those in the know)* in the texts quoted below:

"When you make the two one, and when you make the inside as the outside, and the outside as the inside...[3]"

"The object is related to the subject. The subject is related to the object.

If you want to know these two, their origin is one emptiness.

In one emptiness both are equal, evenly containing innumerable forms.[4]"

"The water-filled pitcher is placed upon water, it has water within and without. It should not be given a name, lest it call forth the error of dualism. Kabir says: "Listen to the Word, the Truth, which is your essence. He speaks the Word to Himself; and He Himself is the Creator.[5]"

We have just gone through four texts from distinct "religious" currents, separated by several centuries and thousands of kilometers. However, for those who grasp the sensitive dimension inside each of them, an astonishing resonance emerges. All these authors describe a relation with God, the Tao, the All, the One, in an identical way, for those who know how to hear it. Proof, if it were needed, that those who tear themselves apart by opposing each other on the outer packaging of the different currents, are unfortunately not getting close to the substance.

---

1. Ibidem
2. Object: anything that, animate or inanimate, affects the senses.
3. Gospel of Thomas 22
4. Daniel Giraud, *Seng T'san: Hsin Hsin Ming*, Arfuyen Edition, 1992
5. *Songs of Kabir*, The Macmillan Company, 1915

The works detailing the texts from which the quoted references are taken are listed in the bibliography, and we can only encourage the reader to read and reread them. This advice may come as a surprise, but as the paradox goes:

"To know and yet (think) we do not know is the highest (attainment); not to know (and yet think) we do know is a disease.[1]"

It warns of the classic error of "knowledge" whose theory is to be avoided. But even in "non-knowledge", the direction to be taken "remains" to be known and understood.

We could have, just as easily, chosen Meister Eckhart, Angelus Silesius, Chuang Tzu, Lieh-Tzu, Hui Neng, Rumi, Ibn Arabi and others, and each time the sensitive dimension expressed would have had the same resonance.

Let us make this echo resonate in us and continue on our way...

---

1. Tao Te Ching 71

Excursion on the Illusory Byways

We should not be pessimistic, or at least not too much. *All that remains* is to accept what has passed, to peel back each layer—familial, societal, religious, philosophical—to arrive at that of the origin of the species, and then "*die while alive*" and this, thanks to the tools of Tradition, to finally experience the "*My God, why have you forsaken me*", torn between the verticality of an ephemeral moment and the horizontality of everyday life. The starting point is to become aware of one's own mediocrity, and to accept it—a vast undertaking...

This should only convince us to keep going, while being careful not to take byways that are not always shortcuts. Very often, too often, one cannot help but be attracted by anything to do with the esoteric, the initiatory, the words that sparkle in our subconscious and hold the promise of an immediate solution. One may find offers of all kinds, more or less serious, and if one frequents the right circles, one may be offered membership of some elitist group.

At that stage, the most important thing is not to fall back into the very misleading traps for the ordinary person, not to take the path of the "Seeker who is constantly seeking" thinking that he is on the Way to the essential. And we know how pleasant it is to take this path, how reassuring it is for the "self" and how safe it is for one's "house".

To avoid this, one must not hesitate to scratch the surface of the layers one has accumulated.

Let us start with the many and varied initiatory societies, whose principles of organization, hierarchy and work actually vary little. The oldest ones were founded around three hundred years ago, based on a syncretism[1] developed

---
1. Syncretism is the sum of influences from different philosophical, religious or esoteric

from various traditional currents.

Today, a whole range of institutions coexist, vying for the largest number of members, legitimacy and possession of the best initiation rites and methods. These institutions have a structure, rules, rituals and principles, as well as a hierarchy linked to the progression of the initiation and, above all, a stereotyped image of the perfect member. Everything is defined, precise and regulated.

Of course, the following are still present—methods of initiation that are supposed to cause a break of the sensitive and allow access to a new sensitive dimension, work on the symbol to open the mind to unsuspected possibilities, a notion of fraternity to succeed in creating an egregore.

But how do things stand in reality?

In all honesty, we are back to a micro society with its own laws, its own accepted format, its own structure, its own internal struggles for power and its own desire for superiority over other groups. We must not confuse an association that aims to carve and insert a stone into a common structure with a path of Awakening, of Union, which necessarily leads to stripping away of the non-essential.

We do not want to create any controversy with this text. There are spiritualities based on humanistic philosophies, which no one can criticize, quite the contrary. But these are far removed from an inner thirst free of any societal consideration. A thirst that can only be quenched through the experience of fusion with God, the Tao, the One. On the one hand, there is "superficial work" through the inclusion of new elements, and on the other, deconstruction to reveal the Profound, "hollowing work".

Of course, the initiation should create a profound rupture in the recipient by bringing into play a trauma of the senses and emotions; but this is often nothing more than a scenario drawn from a manual by guides who obey a learned definition and who take care not to create any psychological shock in the recipient.

---

currents. It is important not to confuse finding the essence of a current in other traditions and syncretism. The latter is often the product of a synthesis of rites, methods and principles drawn from different sources.

We know that in order to reach the Profound, we need to act on the emotions, provoking a fracture in the sensitive state while providing the necessary initiatory element, thereby increasing the field of perception. Theoretically, initiations should be based on these principles, but fear of potential trauma leads to reassuring *(often collective)* initiations, all in a paternalistic spirit. What is more, let us not forget that without daily work with a tool of the Tradition, the initial crack can only be opened with great difficulty, which is what every Tradition affirms.

One often forgets that "*the true circumcision in the Spirit has proved useful in every way*[1]". It is necessary to remind ourselves that the Path to follow is dull, arid and lonely.

Work with the symbol is present, speculating on its various meanings, while remaining in defined thought. In the tests (or trials), it is essential to develop the qualities obtained through belonging to the institution: tolerance, humanism, wisdom, the inner temple to be built. Each new trial is a repetition of these theoretical qualities, which must be present and embellished with a defined symbolic expression. It has to be said that these trials are the means of passing through the levels of the programmed progression.

Logically, the recipient who wants to join the group/institution must copy the way of thinking and the appropriate attitude, in a word "the role", to such an extent that it is very easy to recognize a member of a specific school. Subsequently, the contribution of new elements, the result of precise instruction, enables progression, with rewards as motivation *(as in any society)*.

Clearly, this is a form of conditioning, which is provided to the recipient by persuading him that, thanks to it, he will become superior to what he was *(which may be considered likely)*, or even to ordinary people. So, instead of *"dying in order to be reborn"*, this ends up being a new *"philosophical peel"* designed to reinforce *"the structure of the house"*.

The *"hollowing work"* is a long way off, but the structuring and formative effects are particularly useful to the societal dimension. Of course, in rare cases the culture of fraternity can lead to a genuine dimension of empathy. And work on symbols is indeed a useful first step towards open-mindeness. These are positives. As in every micro-society, there are people with undeni-

---

1. Gospel of Thomas 53

able qualities of the heart, and others who remain in a lowly careerist ideal.

Now, let us take a look at the books on offer on the merchants' stalls.

How to recognize a worthwhile text?

The answer is very simple: "*Trust your intuition!*"

In the books that can be deemed worthy of interest, the experience described, or the consequences thereof, are very often pictorial, peppered with paradoxes where the intellect necessary and useful to everyday life and the intangible absolute clash *(as in the Gospel of Thomas)*, but also sometimes presented with the help of tales *(as in Wu Wei)*, or with interjections that may seem aggressive or pretentious *(Kabir)*, or with notions of the absolute *(Angelus Silesius)*.

But as soon as a text tackles theological, doctrinal, psychological, psycho-analytical or physiological details of differentiation between Awakening and non-Awakening, between "the poor spirit and the Perfect one", one necessarily falls back into "The" trap *(this may also be on purpose, a funhouse mirror to attract the layman; at least sometimes…).*

How to read such works?

It is essential to be driven by an inner revolt that makes it possible to break one's *routine*, result of the comfortable acceptance of ambient conformity *(or the standard offered by the different esoteric, religious or new age movements).*

It can be observed that there is often more spirituality in the story of a life experience than in essays trying to explain the doctrine of a specific religious movement.

One must be utterly uncompromising towards one's greatest enemy — *i.e. oneself* — and also be totally sincere — *and this always towards oneself.*

Are you working for the eyes of others, for your own ego, or for the Other, that is, the primordial spirit, that of the newborn child of Taoism and Christianity, not yet covered in the "different layers of the onion"?

You need to read with your heart, without preconceptions, forgetting theories and intellectual principles. Knowing how to love or reject, with the Profound as your only guide. Naturally, at first, nothing will change, your predefined perspective on things will dictate your pseudo sensitivity. Your opinions will be based on a set of dualistic data, fruit of your conditioning.

But if you accept to listen to the inner voice, silenced since childhood, little by little it may reappear; like a whisper at first, almost inaudible, incomprehensible, made of unfamiliar sensations. Then, by letting it flow without any reservation or mental intervention, it will become distinct, clear and will invade your being. And everything will become obvious, pretensions of all kinds, vested interests, stereotyped reproductions, multicolored parrots.

There is a condition to this, and it is always the same: to use the tools of Tradition to "demolish your house" and thus reconnect.

Let us continue by taking a look at the seminars of various teachings: Far Eastern and exotic spiritualities, all kinds of syncretisms, personal creations following a contact with God (or an awakening, or a relationship with angels), "unstuckers" overcoming psychological blockages, those who communicate with the afterlife, with missing loved ones, with previous lives. It is impossible to list everything. Everyone can believe in what they want or can, this is not the problem, but in order to reach the essence, any additional weight will have to be removed, like an unnecessary peel.

According to basic marketing logic, most sell a product to provide the individual with what he does not have and above all, wishes to have. The list is obvious:

- well-being of all kinds *(psychological, health, vitality)*,
- even better, Happiness with a big H: no more pain or struggle, being happy at all times,
- immortality: the dreamed pre-life and an after-life with all its possibilities, but without the anguish of disappearing,
- a spirituality made of fairy tales: angels who are talking to you; a God of a human dimension who is listening to you; always present and ready to intervene Saints; miracles within your reach,
- an Awakening that will make you a different person, wonderful, admired or even adored, obtaining what others could not acquire, and which, above all, makes you the exception.

Classic manipulation techniques, old as the world, all based on the credulity of the buyer.

There are even more shocking and unacceptable examples: all those who thrive on misfortune.

The misfortune of someone who suffers from the loss of a loved one, a child, or someone with a disease difficult to fight with the available medical means. Everything is offered in this sales niche. But we do not want to be imbued in any way with this darkness, so we will not go further into it, leaving you to observe by yourself what is on offer.

It could be said, *"This is an exaggeration! A particularly pessimistic and negative outlook!"*

So, as a humorous aside, let us look together at the potential *"selling points"* we could glean from the esoteric texts in the previous chapter:

Jesus: *"I will destroy this house, and none shall be able to build it again.[1]"*

Kabir: *"Illusion that men, women and children…"*

Sen Ts'an: *"Gain and loss, right and wrong, abandon all such thoughts at once![2]"*

Lao Tzu: *"The multitude of men all have enough and to spare. I alone seem to have lost everything. My mind is that of a stupid man…[3]"*

The above *"selling points"* would obviously have no success whatsoever in the secular world and are at the opposite of everything previously listed.

Indeed, telling the "potential customer" that it is by becoming as transparent as possible, by asking for nothing, expecting nothing, offering nothing, being nothing, disappearing until that nothing, that he will be able to move forward a little, a tiny bit, and after hours and hours of work with a tool that demands total resignation, maybe one day…

Who would be interested? Honestly?

Most people, certainly not.

And to finish the list of illusory byways, we will touch on "trending spiritualities".

---

1. Gospel of Thomas 71
2. Hsin Hsin Ming
3. Tao Te Ching 20

We have shown the principles used by static religion by indicating the flagrant errors of definition and dogmatism. To avoid those, some go to less familiar terrain which therefore appears more initiatory. We can take Chinese Chan or Japanese Zen as examples. The stripping away of the superfluous is the principle, non-duality the method, emptiness the state. All this is perfect.

But the problem lies in the intellect which, seduced by the discourse, grasps the logic of the method and conceptualizes the principles. This can be true to such an extent that refutation and lack of logic become ready-made answers, a philosophical product, a concept.

Then, with this concept as a support, anything can be intellectualized, even the paradoxical. Awakening becomes *"a truth"* defined in the doctrine.

> *It is for this reason that the Chinese monk Chao-chou (Zhaozhou) answered "Wu!" (the "empty", "the nothing", "the no"[1]) to the koan "Does a dog have Buddha nature or not?", while the Mahayana doctrine, of which he had a perfect grasp, states that "all beings have Buddha-nature"[2].*

With his answer, which was outside all logic, the Master meant that there could be no doctrine, no definition, no logical explanation in the approach to Awakening.

The *Hsin Hsin Ming*, as we have seen, is a compendium of principles to be applied. But in the present deviation, it is transformed into a doctrine and thus becomes a list of truths that are easy to entertain by the intellect.

So it is hardly surprising to see "devising monks" giving lectures to the general public on the theory to be implemented. Explanation, argumentation, questions and answers, in front of an audience easily seduced by the peacock's feathers. Very human.

---

1. Tom Lowenstein, *The Awakening of the Buddha*, Taschen Edition, 2001
2. Author's note: The notion of Wu (translated as "no" as in the Tao Te Ching, for example: Wu Wei = "non-action", but also as "emptiness" or "nothing"). Following Chao-chou's response, the monk Hakuin spent days and nights trying to understand this notion, which led to his awakening, as the story goes.
The best translation of this "nothing" seems to us to be "an undefinable nature", i.e. "the nature of all things", but this should certainly not be understood as "nothing" or "emptiness" in the sense of "absence of everything", since this "nothing" or "emptiness" is part of the All that no words can describe. Wu Wei then becomes "acting according to the nature of things", "naturally" (and not "doing nothing"), just as martial art at a certain level must become "natural", without technique. Moreover, it should be stressed that the reaction to a koan is to "shake" the Profound, not to conceptualize a principle.

Everything becomes stereotypical, "The" blissful smile of circumstance, the displays of humility as a differentiating aspect. It is true that the ordinary person needs to see the uniform in order to respect the other *(whether clothing or some detail, such as pendants, or in attitude and physical appearance)*. This allows to classify the other in a specific mental drawer and assign to him the corresponding status.

The military is well aware of it, as are the justice system and the police force. The modern martial arts have also instituted it, not to mention the various "religious" organisations. Taoism and Sufism had long escaped this trap, but today this no longer seems to be the case.

One can hear extreme speeches held by these followers of Reason, who do not hesitate, not only to affirm absolutes they have never approached, but also constant states of Awakening enabling them to place themselves outside the human realm.

A funny anecdote on this topic: *"One Western Guru used to put a plastic bag on the head of those who claimed to be emotionally detached, even in the presence of mortal danger. And when they had began to suffocate, all without exception struggled, panic-stricken, to remove the bag, the Master laughed and laughed.[1]"*

Theorists of a beautiful theory.

This, of course, has nothing to do with the sacrifice of certain monks, which can only command respect.

But the problem with theory is that it is insipid. It does not matter that the discourse is imbued with the finest supports of the doctrine, it remains lackluster. Not of the usual brilliance of performance, but brilliance of the heart, the witness of lived experience, of the encounter, of an indelible imprint on being.

It is not about attaining an emptiness made of absence, so aptly named in Chan as *"stubborn emptiness"*, but rather a field of consciousness that transcends the individual, that goes beyond all definition and, above all, any doctrine.

So one can only be astonished by remarks like *"the Second Master was defeated in debate"* ("reference" talking about a Chan Master being compared to a Tantric Master). *Vanitas Vanitatum, Omnia Vanitas,* according to another

---

1. Anecdote told by a former student of R.J.

tradition. A very ignorant dimension...

And what is even more amazing is the need these authorities have to check in the texts and verify if the Awakening in question corresponds to the canons, so as not to be mistaken! The doctrine predefines the objective...

There are numerous examples that fall far short of the desired exemplarity.

What we described in this chapter applies to all spiritual circles, although we tried to remain as non-derogatory as possible, so as not to offend anyone's convictions too much.

The list could be very long: Taoism to which Yi King, and Yin and Yang have been added, Gnostic Christianity with its "Bishops" in response to the Roman and the Orthodox, Sufism with its too bookish theory, static religions.

Everything can be intellectualized, explained and supported, based on an analysis that conceptualizes other people's experience *(one can even "win" in debate...)*.

There are too many illusory byways to list. And it is true that it is pleasant to stroll on some of them...

However, let us leave this comfort and get back on track.

The State of Mind to Strive For

Everything we have just shown is aimed at initiating the necessary dismantlement. This is the first step: taking one's conditioning as a working hypothesis, in order to provoke a micro-crack in one's envelope—provided, of course, that this is possible.

Whether you accept or reject some or all of what was explained is of little importance, because what is important is to make all singularities disappear during the Work. For this to happen, it is necessary not to get bogged down in nice theories, and not to have a ready definition of your goal.

Let us take as an example one of the most important paradoxes:

"Wanting without wanting."

Very well, but how to get involved with the entirety of your being in the Work without wanting to do so?

The theory will answer:

"It is enough to let go."

Nice one! Following this type of principle, your vitality will be that of a zucchini, not in a garden, but exposed on a stall. Worthwhile as a tanning session, but not in our case.

Nowadays there is a great confusion regarding the notion of spirituality. The examples provided in contemporary texts and seminars are more reminiscent of a "Disneyland-esque world" and are astoundingly dull and silly. Indeed, you will be told that an individual on the initiatory, religious or awakening path, must be gentle, kind, good, smiling, carefree, humble and generous *(this last point is taught only theoretically once your financial contribution has been received).*

Are you doubtful? Just take a look, the examples abound.

"*And you want me to destroy my house with that!*" you might say. The risk is indeed non-existent. No, it is more like Gandhi's way: "*It is a matter of heart culture, of immeasurable strength. Fearlessness is the first requisite of spirituality.*[1]"

Our Master had another image that was just as "telling":

"*You have to meditate as if there were a tiger in front of you!*"

But it is not a question of being afraid, which would be a normal reaction, nor of imagining oneself brave and invincible. It means that it is essential to wake up, to open one's senses, all senses and heart.

Here we should pause for a moment. Most of the time, and we speak from experience, when you give someone something to work on, as soon as the idea is expressed, the recipient nods and everything is understood *(refer to the notion of definition seen in previous chapters). I understand the meaning of the sentence, put it away in my drawer and that is enough for me.* However, it must be remembered that traditional teachings are "heart-to-heart", using visual, gestural, symbolic and supra-sensory examples; words are quite insufficient. So, it is necessary to "torture" oneself about the meaning of each element encountered instead of being content with the wording describing it.

Opening one's senses requires *subtlety*. The common mistake is to fall into excess — the more extreme a thing is, the more productive it is. A mistake not to be made...

A concrete example. You want to improve your hearing. What do you do? Push the sound to the maximum? Great, you will end up deaf!

On the contrary, it is a good idea to lower the sound and then focus your attention on the slightest variation heard. The more you are immersed in your senses, the more this is productive, but... To reiterate what was said, you must not fall into a state of dullness.

As soon as people are asked to increase their *vitality*, they become more feverish, even aggressive, and lose their sensitivity as a result. There is a paradox here that cannot be understood by intellect alone. As always, it is necessary to have some past references in order to "recover" the state one was in, by calling on one's sensitive memory.

---

1. Gandhi, *La Jeune Inde*, translated by Hélène Hart, Librairie Stock, 1925

To this end, use your imagination, remember an image, then one by one the senses connected to it, relive the situation and finally the resulting emotion (the most important part). From these, "keep" the mental state. It is necessary to repeat the exercise regularly to get the hang of it.

For example:

- a sunrise. You are alone and you feel immersed in your surroundings—nature, air, sound.

- a night, a noise, there is a potential risk *(our Master's tiger)*, your senses are awakened, your whole being is present.

In the Taoist tradition, this is called "*Jingshen*" *(spirit of vitality)* and it includes both *Jing*, the spark of life linked to the breath, and *Shen*, the spirit, or mental, emotional and spiritual activities *(and responses to the stimuli of the "external world")*—often poorly translated as "vitality" alone, which is far too limited.

This is not "letting go" as is often understood, quite the contrary. Not that the term is wrong, at least if the full meaning is taken into account.

The "letting go" must be supported by a "*spirit of vitality*" that amplifies the known senses, as well as "the supra-sensory", at least one can assume as much before experiencing it. This "*letting go*" includes "*wanting without wanting*", which corresponds, as its name suggests, to a thirst of the Profound. This thirst is at the root of an unquenchable inner fire that drives you, in full confidence, to seek an indefinable but anticipated absolute beyond the will of the "self".

At this initial stage, it is essential to make the "*self*" disappear. Without this "*disappearance*" everything undertaken can only be doomed to failure. How to arrive at an absolute while remaining anchored in one's small dimension?

However, the notion is quite simple compared to the actual difficulty of disappearing. As always, theories are nice but very often only strengthen the ego. The gradual erasure of the "self" cannot be done by willpower or a decision, but only by a state of being. Of "*acceptance*". This "*acceptance*", although paradoxical relative to the inner thirst and the "*spirit of vitality*", can be achieved, more or less, through awareness of one's impermanence, one's state of a passer-by, one's illusion—*easier to say than to "be", of course.*

Here again, it is a good idea to look at some real life examples. A simple one first:

- You are going to an interview that you think will be very difficult. When the time comes, it is even worse. Difficult to manage. So, before you do anything, think that everything you are going to experience will soon be only a memory, and that in a few years you will smile at the state in which you were, and if it fails, you will speak about it with derision — *this is not opposed to doing.*

  Making fun of everything (or almost) is a great way to "be a passer-by". Make fun of situations, of serious people (Montesquieu said that solemnity is a fool's delight), of human stupidity, of Know-it-alls, of superficialities, of super-inflated egos, and finally of yourself, which is even easier to do, at least if you do not take yourself too seriously... For some Masters, the best summary of Chan is a burst of laughter.

- Do the same during a long traffic jam, and imagine, while remaining present, the road being empty in a few hours. This will *(maybe)* lead you to think that you yourself will soon only be a memory that you will not be able to share. The importance of your impatience will fade and eventually disappear, losing the weight you have put into it.

Before tackling something difficult it is always a good idea to start with easier things. Trying to jump several steps at once when climbing a staircase can cause one to fall and remain disabled for quite some time.

So, to remain in the appropriate state of mind, be in this acceptance, everything is important and nothing is important *(paradox of our life)*, the thirst to merge is there, allowing to "strive for", but will the door open? Will the Tao welcome you? Today, tomorrow, after tomorrow, in ten years, whatever, one day this will happen, be confident. Accept that this is the case.

This acceptance allows you to relax, to relax your mind. No impatience, no desire, simply be moved by the *"spirit of vitality"*, just as the grass shivers in spring as it reaches for the sky, swayed by the wind — *watch, you will see!*

This relaxation is fundamental, it prevents the mind from being *"stone"*, that is to say *"solid"*, without the possibility of becoming fluid, to penetrate and be penetrated. A *"stone mind"* is rigid, defined, with a contour that limits everything, including its own potential. The definition, the willpower, the constraint, the "non-sensitive" are its consequences.

In martial arts, flexibility is often discussed — making the body more flexible with stretches and gymnastics. But it is suppleness of the mind that one must have for the whole, body/mind, to be supple.

What is more, another fundamental point, relaxation brings the three brains in line, enabling the body to react instinctively and, for our purposes, allows the conscious mind to access, to a greater or lesser extent, the Profound.

A little secret — a simple inner smile can be enough to relax — *but what does it hide?*

Very good. Now it is important to avoid thinking too much.

"*But why?*" one could ask. "*Cogito, ergo sum; I think, therefore I am*" may be the answer. However, the objective is to forget oneself, to blend, and, based on experience, every thought brings one's mind back into the "self" and opposes all communion.

So what to do?

If you are told, "*It is easy!*", well, possibly, but in that case we are close to Chan's "stubborn emptiness". Or you have been lied to, which is more likely and more frequent.

Still, according to the experience of many Seekers, the repetition of a prayer, *Mantra, Dhikr*, etc., in no way prevents thoughts from occurring. Willpower is just as ineffective.

So what to do?

First of all, avoid self-hypnosis, using self-suggestions such as:

- "*I want to have an empty mind!*", something repeated while being convinced of it, accompanied by an illusory desired relaxation.
- "*I am a Master "of such and such", my mind is empty!*", while being convinced of it! — *quite frequent...*

This can put you to sleep partly or completely, causing you to lose all memory afterwards. The result will certainly be an "empty head", where you always think, but without being aware of it!

One can laugh about it, but many meditators are at that level. The Chan expression "stubborn emptiness" was coined for a reason, and when one meets meditation practitioners of all stripes, one cannot help but be amazed at the confusion that exists on the subject.

Indeed, in many meditation-based practices, the primary obsession is to be "here and now", to be free of disruptive thoughts, in complete relaxation. Very well, and then... back to the doctrine.

Regarding *"non-thought"*, time is without doubt the best solution. When the *"presence of the breath"* becomes tangible, the mind will be *"taken"* by it. Just as the *"presence of God"* in certain spiritual practices, idealized and mental, may enable the absence of thoughts—*but where is the difference?*

Pending this state, several principles are proposed by authentic Traditions:

- As soon as a thought appears, imagine that you throw it into the fire that is your mind.
- As soon as a thought appears, produce a mental interjection, a silent cry, for example: *"Peh!"*
- Let thoughts pass like clouds, not stopping at any one.
- And above all, do not attach importance to *"non-thought"*, because it will become a singularity.

At this point, we would like to allow ourselves a small digression.

Everything examined above must lead to what is called: "*The motionless mind.*" For the ordinary person this means a mind that does not move and is therefore lifeless—*the perfect image of "stubborn emptiness"*.

One Japanese monk, Takuan, spoke of a mind that is not attached to anything. And being unattached, motionless, it can attach itself to everything.[1]

How to understand such a paradox?

Imagine a pond, a classic image. If it is agitated, if you dive into it to follow a young frog *(or a young toad)*, the swirls will cause the reflections of the pond's surroundings to become blurred, elusive, or even seemingly non-existent.

A motionless pond shows the correct reflection of everything, allowing to see any detail, and is therefore the opposite of immobility through immobility. Just like the motionless mind.

---

1. Takuan, *Mystère de la sagesse immobile*, Shibata, Albin Michel 1987

This is one answer, but stopping at an answer, however "attractive", is mental immobility.

It is obvious to any reader that the pond is our mind and that the swirls are due to our mental activity *(our basic instincts, our conditioning, our thoughts, our concerns, etc., not to mention our ego in the sense of our envelope)*, which prevents us from perceiving the proper "reflection" of things.

But, unlike the awakened ones of modern Buddhism, it is not "enough" to "empty" one's mind.

Why is that?

Have you asked yourself the following question: what is the reflection? Is this your vision of things? Or something else?

Indeed, this is the entirety of your perceptions. Your senses.

Is that all? What else is there?

There is also everything that is "sensitive" in you, including empathy with what surrounds you: people, animals, trees, nature, everything.

You do not feel anything?

Yet there is no difference between you and others, between you and the Other.

Your perception may even go beyond what you feel today, the supra-sensory.

By gradually removing the swirls, you can improve your "perception". Then, progressively, like during rehabilitation, your perception will become more "sensitive" and will "overflow" into other spaces. *(With time, patience and thanks to a "method of rehabilitation")*

But what is the nature of all these perceptions?

It is your field of consciousness, your consciousness. It can expand and expand, and one day the center will disappear for a moment, forever.

Very often, texts stop at this level. But there is one essential point still missing: *"Intention."* As always, the word is not enough.

Firstly, it must be said that no intention can exist without preceding *"attention"*. The latter consists in bringing one's field of consciousness to a particular place or direction, *"extending"* one of the senses toward the place or direction. It is possible, of course, to combine several senses at the same time.

Two examples:

- I keep my attention on my hand or on my arm, on my legs, or even my entire body. The last is only achievable "tangibly" after a long work. This attention is at the tactile level and vision can be added.
- I keep my attention in one direction, this could be sight, hearing, smell, the sense of touch can be added. If the sense of touch is added in the chosen direction, this is intention. It is also possible to emit in this direction the "driving element" of my body, as if moving, but without actually moving.

Here is an example: withdrawing one's hand just as the other is about to shake it, will create a kind of void in the other. This void is the intention to move.

As we will see later, the thirst to go towards God is another example of intention, but one that is linked to a different fundamental element: the heart.

A quick aside: "Do you know why the wedding ring is placed on the fourth finger?" Most people obey traditions without seeking their meaning. The answer is "because it was thought that the vein of the heart arrived there". And our beloved scientists have proven that this is ridiculously wrong. Yet, how is Christ's blessing depicted on Orthodox icons? His hand forms a fourth finger mudra. A place that favors the breath of the heart. The Heart is the universal symbol of the sensitive dimension of love, vector of the Breath…

If we point our heart in a direction, linking all our senses, we realize that we are linked to compassion, and even, for the most sensitive, empathy. The latter, unlike compassion, which is often the result of instilled morality, is a genuine state attained through union with the person on whom we have focused our intention/attention — *in China there is a word to define this attention/intention — Yi. Shen being the mind, Xin the heart.*

Finally, in conclusion of this chapter, do not ask for the impossible. If in everyday life you perform shallow, petty acts, if you reduce everything to your personal interest, if your generosity stops at the fear of a hypothetical future, it means that your mind is caught in a very solid, even unbreakable, shell.

So, begin by changing a little bit.

Otherwise, no tool or guide will be able to do anything for you.

The Tools

Once the work of "deconstruction" mentioned in the previous chapter has been undertaken, it is quite natural to move to its "active" phase, which offers the possibility of connecting oneself using the "breath".

It is necessary to remember though that without the "right state of mind" the tools will not work. The entirety of the previous chapter was to explain this. Too often, reproach is addressed to the one who transmits, to the tools provided, while the only person responsible and one's greatest enemy is oneself.

You can have all possible tools, but without the right state during their use, nothing can be achieved. A guard can keep still for hours, while remaining vigilant (here and now), a pool player can be present in the action with total concentration and an empty mind, but is that enough?

The tools of the Tradition make it possible to contemplate the loss of one's individuality, something reason cannot accept. Guided by the "survival instinct", the ego will do everything in its power to avoid that loss.

Hence the importance of understanding how we function at the level of our instinct (the three brains), our "self", and why a spiritual awakening using the intellect is impossible.

It is therefore necessary to activate this link to the Absolute, which goes through our interiority and then make it disappear in God, in the Tao, in the One, whatever one wants to call it.

But contrary to what is often taught, the interiority we are talking about is not obtained by reading and rereading sacred texts, or by respecting a formal doctrine and performing defined rituals. It requires a dissolution of one's presence after one's sensitive dimension has been amplified consciously.

This paradox, connected to the evolution of the "breath within oneself" and its relation with the "undifferentiated breath" *(primordial or universal)*, can only be understood through experience.

The following maxim sums it up quite well:

"If you only look inside yourself, you will not find, if you only look outside, you will not find either.[1]*"*

What are these tools?

First of all, we can say with certainty that the tool we will present makes it possible to become aware of the "breath". Our experience and those of others confirm it. This book is not about developing an abstract theory but about tangible work.

No false promises though; without consistent work, without personal effort, without perseverance, nothing will happen. But with time and patience, the tool will become, little by little, a haven of peace, offering you the possibility to connect with the essence hidden within you. Your thirst will increase and your "envelope" will become more and more porous. This permeability will transform your state of being. It will gradually pass, as Paul of Tarsus specified, from the state of *psuchikos* to that of *pneumatikos*. The "Breath" will no longer be an allegory but will become "substance", support of a shared but unique consciousness.

And one day, if the door opens, if the Tao welcomes you, this thirst can be quenched for an eternal moment that will transform you forever.

Is it better to make people dream, by promising the development of each individual's potential through simple, pleasant methods, or daily happiness through effortless meditation and self-suggestion techniques, or even easier, to suggest that a hypothetical initiation will bring about a new dimension in just a few dozen minutes?

Everyone is free to take the path they want, but it always must be done with "profound sincerity", as Sufi Yusuf Hamadani said:

"The superior experience and knowledge will be made available to a man or woman in exact accordance with his worth, capacity and earning of it. Hence,

---

1. Oral tradition of Master WXJ.

if a donkey sees a melon he will eat its rind; ants will eat whatever they can get hold of; man will consume without knowing that he has consumed.

Our objective is to achieve, by the understanding of the Origin, the Knowledge which comes through experience.

This is done, as with a journey, only with those who already know the Way.

The justice of this state is the greatest justice of all: because, while this knowledge cannot be withheld from him who deserves it, it cannot be given to him who does not deserve it.

It is the only substance with a discriminating faculty of its own, inherent justice.[1]*"*

We should not lie to ourselves.

Every day, every moment, seek, and as soon as you can, work to move forward. It will be trying, daunting, it can plunge you into doubt, you will have to face yourself, but without these trials, nothing can be achieved.

Accompaniment by an experienced person may be useful.

And, of course, any disturbance felt should not only lead to an immediate cessation of the practice, but also to a consultation with a medical professional.

The tool: "to be led to the center"

This tool is the fruit of the Taoist tradition and is more than three thousand years old. However, we are not about to embark on a compilation of contemporary works on Taoism. You will find its theoretical developments easily; they express what scholars have drawn from the writings in their possession. However, the secret is the culture of this tradition, the understanding of the terms used, as well as of the many metaphors describing the details of the work to be undertaken.

Taoism, based on empirical principles and transmitted "heart to heart", has been transformed into a sophisticated theory onto which other traditions have been grafted, such as the Yin and Yang, the five elements, Shamanism, thus forming a complex whole made of magic and idolatry. The convoluted often hiding a lack of depth in knowledge.

In what follows, only the tradition received "heart to heart" will be de-

---

1. Idries Shah, *Wisdom of the idiots — Sufi Stories*, E.P. Dutton and Co., 1971

scribed, as well as the resulting experiential knowledge.

You must first choose a convenient time in your day that will allow you to fully immerse yourself in the tool. In a quiet place, without other people, if possible. If you are lucky enough to be in the countryside, going outside will be more pleasant, otherwise choose your cellar or a closed room.

Position yourself in front of a tree, or if you are inside, in front of any object or representation to which you feel attracted, as if in harmony. If it is a tree, it must feel "alive", "connected" to you.

Place yourself at a distance of 2 to 3 meters from the chosen "object".

As in the drawing above, position yourself: standing, feet parallel, separated by a distance of about fifty centimeters: legs neither tense, nor bent; back straight without tension; head as if suspended; arms on the side of the body; forearms slightly bent forward; hands as if lying flat on a table; fingers directed forward.

If you are sick or disabled, use the same position for the torso and arms but sitting. The lying position requires special preparation.

Your entire body is like grass in the spring *(example provided in the previous chapter)*, as if carried by a natural flow that travels through it.

Release the chest, shoulders, belly, straight spine traversed by this flow.

Your attention, perception, is first of all inside the body. The latter is "hollow", you put your mental presence *(sensitive/awareness)* inside it and maintain it.

You look at the "object" in front of you with your gaze going beyond, as if crossing it, without staring at it, but still seeing it.

Your sense of touch does the same with your fingertips extending to the object and beyond; you perceive it in a sensitive way. Thus, your inner presence extends to the object and even beyond.

There may be a certain difficulty to "extend towards" due to all the blockages and conditioning that cover our natural momentum.

So what to do?

As always, take examples from your lived experience. The best, in our eyes, is a day when, after an absence considered too long, you opened your arms towards a loved one: your child, your partner, your parent, your friend.

This moment, devoid of any material interest, any voluntary intention, any speculation, where time is as if suspended, where you already make one with the other, must be "relived" in its entirety.

It is very simple, provided you have experienced it. These are exceptional moments, especially if the sensitive perception of their impermanence leads to an amplified awareness. Extending towards, with all your heart.

You amplify your "spirit of vitality" which exalts your senses both inside and from the inside to the "*object*", so it all makes "one".

Above all, do not be mentally or physically tense, only maintaining the "presence" is important. Tend towards the state described in the previous chapter, in relaxation, with confidence and serenity.

Start with a quarter of an hour, to then arrive at one hour a day. And, whenever you can, periodically, do three hours a day, spaced or not.

Do not think, let go, nothing is important, release all tension, forget the tool and yourself, hold "The presence". Only the latter should maintain your awareness.[1]

Over time, you will feel something like a pressure inside the body, first in the arms, then towards the chest, then gradually in the legs. Whenever you get this feeling, do not focus on it. Any attention paid, any desire to discover a phenomenon, blocks any possible evolution.[2]

---

1. Examples similar to this type of work in other traditions:

Chi Kong: The aim is to circulate the energy through the meridians, towards the chakras, to improve well-being and to preserve health. The problem is that any definition limited to oneself during the work pre-defines the result or the pseudo-result (self-hypnosis). What is more, any egocentric objective is limited by one's own mediocrity of thought and to one's interiority. One must be broad-minded, generous, beyond oneself, expanding to forget oneself and opening up to connect.

Martial arts: Two possibilities. 1) Work more or less similar to the one presented, but with the egocentric goal to become more efficient and stronger. And yet somehow the resulting force should be used to overcome one's own limits. 2) Neuro-tendinous work, so limited that there is no point in discussing it. Even "beating the drum", which is the vibration of breath, is reduced to a febrile vibration of the body. An impoverishment due to not having touched the essence.

2. There are trends. For example, *Hara Tanden (or Dantian in Chinese)* so dear to the Japanese that it led to the publication of a large number of books. Following them, practitioners from various disciplines worked to focus on a point in their belly. However, any attention maintained on a single point limits the breath in this spot and keeps it there.

It is fundamental to remember that you are moving towards a perception not yet known, any preconception will limit your future field of consciousness.

Do not think, forget, let yourself be carried away, extend towards the *"object"* with your entire being, exalt your mind without feverishness, with calm and confidence, and let it be. Arouse an inner smile to guide your self-derision.

One day, after hours upon hours of consistent work, you will have the feeling that this pressure escapes from your fingertips. The pressure inside the body will be more flexible, more malleable. Do not seek it, it will happen by itself.

You will find that it fluctuates with your *"spirit of vitality"*. The more the latter increases, the more the pressure increases and the more it escapes. The Breath is like a *"fluid"*.

The problem at that point is that your *ego/persona* will become satisfied with the result, and you will either become self-satisfied, or you will want to show off. Another pitfall. You will bring your consciousness back to you, and any further evolution will become impossible *(just as every thought brings consciousness back to the self)*.

Moreover, at this stage, theBbreath only comes out if it has connected in a subtle way, with attention, a flexible and light intention. Otherwise, like a valve closing under pressure, your relation with the outside, your permeability, instead of improving, will regress. The breath will be in compression and therefore useless at the level of the Spirit, although it will be usable at the level of the body, allowing for capabilities much greater than the muscular or neuro-tendinous ones. This is certainly why some "Wise men" say that the *Masters of internal martial arts* are not fully accomplished — *with the exception of those who follow a spiritual path in parallel, ending up forgetting their initial objective, or even any objective.*

Let us pause for a moment and clarify a couple of things.

First of all, the proposed tool allows a real-world approach to the *"Breath"*. For this to happen, the Breath must become "tangible" *(sensitive awareness)*

Indeed, the Hara is used here, but this is to be done "naturally", just like the opening of the chakras and "the rest". But all of this is unimportant in the face of the Tao or God (it still brings back to oneself).

and the work must be done on a felt inner *"matter (substance)"*. It is very difficult to engage in this type of work without going through these stages of sensitive perception. Otherwise it would be like *"trying to sculpt the wind"*—*possible, but with the risk of an evolution towards a waking dream.*

Second clarification concerning the Work. The work in progress is you. The Guide who uses this tool is still you. The Work is similar to a work of Art, your instinct guides you. Just like the Chinese poet Gia Ki indicated that "*The poem is the sound of the heart!*", the tool must resonate in the same way, with your heart, your sensitive state, your thirst for the Profound. These must guide you, do not lose them along the way!

And always remind yourself of what Mencius said:

"*He who attends to his greater self becomes a great man, and he who attends to his smaller self becomes a small man.[1]*"

Let us continue.

At a certain stage of the practice, your awareness of the "Breath" inside the body will give you the feeling of extending towards the object. The common mistake at that point is to accentuate with force and willpower the intention that guides "the matter (substance)" towards the object. A mistake because it is the will of the "self" that acts. Obvious, but very common.

On the contrary, you must "lower the sound"—*see previous chapter*—and amplify your sensitivity, as if to hear "an almost inaudible whisper".

Then, over time, the "Breath" becomes more malleable, the slightest variation of your sensitive state makes it vary.

In this perception of what we can begin to call "Breath", four states can be distinguished. Based on the "primordial tradition":

- solid: a stagnant breath, more or less
- liquid: the breath is moving but is in weak communion
- gaseous: breath connected with the undifferentiated breath
- etheric: breath that has fused with the primordial breath *(connected to the Spirit)*

Note: your relation with the "object" at the gaseous stage becomes sensitive, like

---

1. Henri Borel, *L'esprit de la Chine,* La main courante, 2007

it is a part of you, not through conceptualization, but because it is felt that way.[1]

One discovers that "*the Breath becomes the vector of expansion of one's consciousness*".

Remember what Seng Ts'an said:

> "*The subject follows when the object ceases,*
> *The objects is expelled when the subject sinks.*
> *The object is related to the subject*
> *The subject is related to the object.*"

Surprisingly precise, is it not? — *the meaning/direction of "object" is multiple, of course.*

The *"Breath"* then becomes permanently present. When you walk, when you make a gesture, it is inside you and outside. It carries you, it condenses, expands, according to your own emotional and sensitive fluctuations. It exists without your will, but it can also vary according to it. A very disturbing paradox, where the "Profound" emerges in an obvious way.

We could also mention here that the Taoist notion of "*breathing with the feet*" is not a metaphor but a reality of the "Breath". Just ask yourself about the benefit of the Buddhist "lotus position". We see the initial four main sensors of breath: the palms of both hands and the two soles of the feet. Visible, for example, in Tara *(a Buddhist deity)*, but also in Christ's wounds — *the "error" of representing the crucifixion with nails located in Jesus' palms would therefore not be one, but rather an indication meant for initiates.*

Additionally, because the "Breath" leads to a modification of the field of consciousness, other phenomena are to be noted. "Sight" is modified, the supra-sensory perception of the "object", whatever it may be, supplementing vision; all life is perceived in a sensitive, "holistic" manner, the animal, the tree, the blade of grass. Sounds become surprisingly "tangible". Empathy increases in parallel, not through moral analysis, but because the sensitive state of the other is shared, amplifying emotion. Consequently, it becomes necessary to move away from everything that is felt as unpleasant.

What has just been described is shared by most of those who follow the

---

1. Further clarification: remember that the Neocortex enables "recognition of the object as an external reality in a given space". At this stage, we can speak of a change in the Seeker's state, moving from egocentrism to allocentrism, in line with the Taoist concept of man as "part of the Universe" rather than "center of the Universe".

path. This is not a doctrine, but the observation of a natural transformation. One wonders whether the metaphor of leaving paradise after tasting the fruit of the Tree of knowledge of Good and Evil — *i.e. the baby gradually taking on its human nature, then the sexual one, and using its binary analysis of everything* — does not correspond to the metaphor of the link connecting it in awareness with God, the Tao, the One.

A real transmutation of the being must occur, but we prefer to call it a return to the initial sensitive state, to one's profound nature.

In time, this *"permeability to the Breath"* expands, reaching all pores of the skin. Once opened, the door will no longer close — *this is confirmed by the esoteric tradition.*

In Chinese, it is called "to open the door of ghosts". It is an opening of the field of consciousness that can lead to a perception of "what escapes the ordinary person". This topic requires the advice of an informed individual.

And then? What do we do with the (pseudo) performance achieved?

"What is the point!", one might think. Indeed, is this state actually useful?

Of course, we could speculate by saying that this presence is that of God, the Tao, which may or may not confirm the One. And then settle for the "answer". Why not? It will be different for each person. But for some, the horizon is yet to be reached. Will it ever be? As its name suggests, probably never, and that is certainly its appeal.

If this *"presence"* is deemed insufficient, if it induces a more imperious inner thirst, provoking an even stronger fire within oneself, making the perceived union essential, then all that remains is to truly *"fade away"*. The only remaining solution, according to Tradition, is to rely *"on God's will to open the door for us"*, *"on the Tao to welcome us"*.

At that point, the final and most difficult obstacle is to "erase" oneself sufficiently so as to disappear.

One must become smaller than small, erase oneself even further, lose even this *"spirit of vitality"* that has breathed us, lose one's presence, lose the reflection of the "spirit of individuality", to then join the indefinable.

This cannot be created, it is not a theatrical play, nor the fruit of one's imagination. One day, you are using the tool, not for any reason, but to escape your own dimension, to seek refuge. And maybe:

"The tenuous barrier that separated you suddenly breaks, you cross the object to go beyond it, and at the same time, you absorb the All in you and burst towards this All, and you are aware of this All, as if suspended in time, everywhere and nowhere. You are undivided consciousness, without the "self"."

But this is only one person's sensitive expression, yours will be what it will be, do not pre-define it, as it can only anchor you inside the limits of your intellectual understanding.

And when one returns, you find footing in a dimension that seems very mediocre to you. But that is how it is.

How long did it last? A second, an hour, a century, everything was suspended, you do not know. But your surroundings immediately bring you back to your own dimension.

The memory left, is it *"reality"*, or what we were able to *"bring back"* from this experience, what we were able to perceive according to the limits of our consciousness, what was offered to us. The answer is not too important, but having been relieved of our own *"being"* is a wonderful memory that cannot but make us nostalgic.

This consciousness of the One, this fusion with the Tao, this absorption by God, is liberation, far superior to any earthly realization, but does it even make sense to compare?

Afterwards, you avoid talking about it except to those who are on the path. People believe you kindly, question this perception, think of a hallucination, quote texts in response, but all this does not really matter and is immediately swallowed up by the memory of your experience.

What is this lived experience?

"This equilibrium of the moment, this suspension of the instant where nothing is decided, nothing is created, where time stops time, a relative state, not yet an act, not yet completed, neither in consistency nor in direction.

State that can be material or immaterial, object or thought waiting for multiple but unique definitions; the whole suspended in its impermanence.

The impermanent becoming permanent in a simultaneously fleeting and infinite moment, thus breaking all opposition, all duality, all definition, because everything can become All, the All being a single consciousness.[1]"

You know "your" truth, your facet of the Absolute.

And your future will offer, in response to your quest, a particular facet.

Our description of the work to be carried out is complete.

Simple? Only in appearance. Your biggest obstacle, your biggest enemy, is yourself, you will see. And *"it"* will use all means to fight your thirst, all. Excuses to do something else, desires for easier, more rewarding, more enjoyable distractions, feelings of uselessness, feelings of illusion, *"what for?"*, *"what is the point?"*. The struggle will often seem unequal and "rightly so".

A piece of advice, if luck puts a guide on your path, do not follow him, this is not his role, at least if he is honest and experienced. His duty is to show you the direction to follow, to help you avoid dead ends. But it will be up to you to walk the path, alone.

Of course, the tool is important, but make sure that it does not supplant the Work. If it does, then it can only be used to "pass the time" or worse, to validate the one using it.

This is more common than you think. Simply look with "a sincere eye" at the careerism of most of those who work in initiatory or Awakening spiritualities. The greatest enemy remains the "self".

The most difficult to obtain is not the tool itself—*at least not always*—but *"the right way to use it"* and *"the right state"* for the Work to be accomplished.

The tool: "prayer"

The best example of a tool offered to a large number of people is certainly "the prayer". Under all heavens, in all religions, people pray. Most often, a very human thing, people pray to implore.

To whom is this prayer addressed?

A God, a higher authority, an intermediary who can accommodate one's request. This can range from personal interest, or that of a loved one, at the material level, to that essential for survival. We can certainly understand the inner impulse that drives a person to seek "outside" help, especially when the aim is to bring relief from "suffering".

---

1. expression based on the author's experience

Does prayer have an influence on the course of things? Does this influence partly justify monastic life, which is outside the afflictions of ordinary life? Some people think so. Thoughts certainly have a life of their own, as we are trying to prove it nowadays; do those expressed during prayers have influence on the current of events, on external thoughts, on any living element? It is plausible.[1]

But that is not the type of prayer that interests us.

Let us move on to those that can be considered a tool, with the function of creating immanence in order to move towards a potential transcendence.

The postures of prayer

There are several, according to the sources. Some examples:

- Standing, on one's knees or sitting, the palms of one's hands clasped in front of the face.

- Standing, the palms of one's hands clasped in front of the face or above the head. Bust straight or inclined.

- On one's knees, prostrating towards the ground with hands on either side of the head.

- On one's knees, arms outstretched on each side of the body, palms towards the sky.

- Lying down or sitting, by necessity.

- No posture, when the Profound requires it.

The statement of the prayer

- According to a defined text.

- According to a defined ritual.

- Out loud, in a low voice, with a whisper, silently.

---

[1]. The principle of the relativity of time is not well understood by ordinary people. Some Buddhist schools specify that "it is not the water that flows under the bridge, but it is the bridge that advances over the water". That is to say, time is a lure, everything exists at the same time, only our consciousness of the moment travels through it. We can take film as an example, only the projected image is visible at the level of our consciousness, however at the level of the support the previous images still exist, same as the following ones already exist (and all are present if the experiential "fusion" exists: "suspended time"). But this does not change the fact that, when one has to "jump into the water", at that moment, the effort remains to be made. This paradox is not obvious to everyone.

- According to one's own form, one's own text, one's own ritual. *"If you don't find a prayer that suits you, invent one!"* Saint Augustine

In the direction

- Of a symbol.
- Of a place.
- Of the connection felt: sky, tree, sea, or any other.

We recall the remark made at a conference by an old "initiate" who objected to the use of the word "heart" to indicate the sensitive realm. He said, with all the certainty of his intellect, "The heart is an organ that conducts blood through the body and has no other function!" And yet, all traditions use this symbol the world over, from time immemorial. Also recall these popular expressions: "heart to heart", "put heart into the work", "love with all your heart", "mudra of the heart".

Is the sensitive expression of Breath linked to the Spirit more present there? Certainly, when the "permeability" of the body allows it.

"Praying is not asking. It is a longing of the soul." said Gandhi. It is "in this right state of mind" that the communion is fore-sought; *"wanting without wanting", "extending towards", "accepting", "submitting oneself"*.

When your inner impulse is carrying you, an answer may be offered to you.

Did you notice something?

Yes, there are surprising similarities with the previous tool:

- Same state. Same principles.
- Same inner attention: recollection, presence.
- Same impulse towards *(intention)*: symbol, direction, place.
- Same beyond: beyond the symbol, beyond the direction, beyond the place, union.
- Same intensity: fervor of prayer.
- Same forgetting oneself: the inner impulse is directed, love.
- Same non-definition: God is indefinable, same as the Tao, the One.

Proof, if necessary, that the essence of all traditions is identical. But in the case of prayer, except for the rare people who devote their lives to this search (monks), the time spent in prayer is not enough to create the matter/substance of the "breath".

In the Hesychast way, one is told to pray without interruption — same as among the Sikhs, where meditation on God must also become permanent — the prayer of the heart in the Orthodox tradition has this same function — in this tradition, it is said that "to breathe is to pray". Endless prayer that tends to develop a "state", a modification of "sensitive perception".

Indeed, work with the tool can be compared to the rehabilitation of a lost function. People have lost awareness of the "Breath" within them, as well as the relation — *what we might call the "supra-sensory"* — with what surrounds them. As a result, this sense is totally atrophied, and the difficulty lies in reactivating it. All the tools of Tradition have this function; the means vary, but the overall method remains the same:

- Awakening the sense by removing parasites (disturbing thoughts, sounds, sights, etc…) and increasing one's *"spirit of vitality" — one's sensitive dimension.*
- Enhancing the perception and function of this sense.
- Through it, increasing the presence of "Breath".
- Making it more "fluid" inside the body.
- Making it "alive".
- At the same time, improving one's "relation" with the outside world.
- Establishing the conscious junction of "Breath" between inside and outside — the *"primordial breath".*

Again, the four states of the Tradition: solid, liquid, gaseous, etheric; or in other words: earth, water, air, fire.

All while forgetting the objective, paradox of paradoxes.

But nothing can replace experience, the objective of this text is only to indicate a direction.

One has to be very patient, the initial awareness of the *"Breath"* in the entirety of the body is more or less long depending on the individual. Then, there is a long work of "transformation of the Breath", which will allow to voluntarily guide it inside the body and then link it outwards.

Finally, the mind is called upon to "melt into the breath" and commune, even unite, with the *"undifferentiated breath"*.

Breath is consciousness, is Spirit.

Here, in simple words, we see the Taoist principle of Jing, which guides the breath (Chi, Qi), and then the whole binding to Shen (spirit) to open up to the Tao. It is up to everyone to translate this into the words of their Tradition.

The tool: "the sound"

According to the same principle, the breath can be driven by sound. Several traditions use this method:

The Mantra — or *"tool of the spirit"*, *"protection of the spirit"* — is not, as is often understood, a "magic formula", but a tool of accomplishment.

The contemporary trends lead to a variety of interpretations of what mantra is. Some claim potential miraculous effects thanks to a connection with some divinity, others insist on the virtues of the Tibetan pronunciation, forgetting that in China the sound is completely different and that often the very meaning of the words has been forgotten — *it is important to point out that at a certain level the Mantra can be performed silently.*

Always the finger and the Moon.

The Mantra is a tool that, through sound, guides the Breath inside the body along a determined path, so that it can finally "explode" to the outside and potentially connect with the "undivided breath". It should be noted that the more the Breath becomes "fluid" and then "gaseous", the more effective the Mantra is.

Of course, nowadays, Mantras are chanted melodiously to attract the layman, but that is another topic. An often repeated theory is that the tireless repetitions aim to stop all thought; unfortunately, as is often the case, the precise work of the "Breath" is forgotten.

The reason for this is always the same. To guide the Breath with the sound, the perception of its "substance" must be present. To that effect, it is very helpful to link this practice to a meditation aimed at gaining awareness of the "Breath" — *awakening of the "sense"*. This is a tradition known from experience.

This notion of experience means that it is possible to recognize other traditions that combine sound and Breath. When ones knows the essence of one Tradition, all other authentic ones are recognized.

To name a few others:

"Dhikr"— *"remembrance of God"* or *"practice that revives this memory"*. Here also, it is necessary to be able to distinguish between what is intended to attract the layman in the form of melodies and what activates the "internal Breath". Some are of a striking intensity and emotionally impressive.

Other tools for working with the "Breath" using sound exist or have certainly existed, judging by the principles of sound emission that can be observed.

For example:

- "diphonic songs" from Mongolia—*called "khôômii"*, from Tibet—*"dbyangs"*, *"vowels" in Tibetan*, from Asia or India—*nowadays there are many songs recorded and intended for sale. In Mongolia, for example, some have become disco songs.*

- "singing while holding a needle between the lips"- *where the current idea is to compete; the one who bleeds loses.*

- "Gregorian chants" at their origin—*one can assume.*

The tool: "the art of the movement"

Just like sound, movement of the body can also guide the "Breath".

The principle is identical to that of the first tool described—*to be led to the center.* It consists in *"connecting oneself to the object"*—*the object can become virtual over time.* The perception of the "Breath" is as usual progressive, increasing over time. But there is a prerequisite for this related to the initial awakening of the sense. It must be stressed that it is at the very least extremely difficult, even impossible, to achieve awakening using only this tool.

Any movement, for the ordinary individual, is activated by "a deliberate intention" that puts to sleep both the perception and the application of the "Breath". Remember that willpower— *"to want it"*—has no hold over the Profound, so any movement, even slow, will therefore remain a consequence of this habitual "deliberate intention". It is therefore necessary to call upon an unknown "something else". The entire method will therefore consist in "deceiving this automatism", this mode of action, in order to activate "another command", which is partly atrophied.

There is often confusion on this last point. For the layman, the outer appearance remains the same, the movements are slow, dense (neuro-tendinous and isometric), aesthetically pleasing (unimportant at the level of the tool), but the "Breath" is not activated. A mime knows how to reproduce a dense movement, just as a guard knows how to remain still.

The same issue is also found in contemporary Hatha Yoga, where practitioners strive after physical performance, always focusing on appearance.

This is a difficult endeavor, which requires a very precise, often surprising progression, relative to the degree of perception of the "Breath" by the recipient. Tradition, wisely, combines the first tool mentioned, "to be led to the center", and that of the movement. The first offers the necessary awakening of the "Breath", as long as the tradition is respected, of course.

Awareness of the "Breath" makes it possible to guide it with movement, circulating it in each part of the body, while remaining connected to the external "object". Each movement must have neither beginning nor end and be connected to both the one that precedes it and the one that follows it, everything being movement—*immobility is movement, a paradox based on experience.* All without the desire of "pure force". It is necessary to feel like being bathed in a very dense sea, with the liquid both outside and inside.

"Take a pitcher full of water and set it down in the water—now it has water inside and water outside." Kabir

Vigilance is required for a long time to avoid creating a mental opening in the movement, which would break the connection with the "Breath".

However, as progress is made, the intention and attention that are initially part of the method, must fade to give way to the natural. But this is no ordinary natural, it is a new sense, that of the "Breath". All of which enables one to produce more force than one could using the muscular and neuro-tendinous systems.

At this stage, it is possible to make a "big exhale of breath" on an opponent through the production of significant force, or even to create in him a disturbance of the internal Breath. But stopping here limits the work done to the mediocrity

of a very relative result.

Every movement thus corresponds to an inhalation and an exhalation of the "Breath" that is gradually felt by all pores of the skin.

"The Spirit must become substance and this substance must become form."
Oral tradition of Master WXJ

Over time, following the principles received, the subject disappears to become a link to the "undifferentiated breath", his mind connected in awareness.

At this stage, any action is not of the will of the "Self" but of the "Other" who takes control. This "Other" has a dimension that escapes the "Self", because the latter's limitations prevent it from having the quality needed for this bond.

This splitting of the mind allows the "Self" to accept to "leave its place to the Other", the latter consciously taking control of the movement. Which is reminiscent of Kabir:

"Him whom I went out to seek, I found just where I was: He now has become myself whom before I called "Another"!"

Finally, we should also mention:

The tool: "respiration"

This tool is probably the most confusing of all. Breathing and "Breath" can only lead one to think that breathing is "Breath", i.e. one and the same thing. A very common mistake, both in the many translations and interpretations of esoteric texts and in those dealing with the Tool.

Yet, the physiological breathing essential to our survival can, consciously or unconsciously, lead the subtle "Breath". Just like movement, sitting meditation, standing meditation, *Asanas, Mantras, Dhikr, Pranayama,* all would only have a very limited physiological and mental dimension if the link with "Breath" did not exist.

In the authentic tradition of Yoga, it is said, as previously mentioned, that *Asanas* make it possible to gain awareness of the "Breath" and that *Pranayama* allows to guide it. The latter tool uses the attention and intention of inspiration, exhalation and retention to guide the "Breath".

There are many books dealing with this topic. Choosing a good one is all the more difficult. That is why we discussed the nature of the writings in a previous chapter.

The complexity of the techniques, such as meditation positions, sound principles, breathing processes, movement methods, can also become a sneaky trap.

Diversity and Unity of the Tools

How many practitioners become experienced "technicians" capable of dissecting every detail, explaining the significant differences between schools and currents, often concluding that theirs is the truth?

How many students go to the ends of the earth to learn new positions, new techniques, and tirelessly pursue performance for years on end?

As the well-known proverb goes, it is necessary to look at the moon and not at the finger pointing at it. Masters worthy of the name arrive at a state where "everything is technique: or, the paradoxical equivalence that "technique does not exist".

The navel-gazing of performance, the cult of character, are attractive but lock people in the same dead ends as those created for ordinary people in society. Again, the packaging changes but remains omnipresent.

It is not a question of being a practitioner, a "technician", of becoming an expert, or a master, but of using a tool for its function, which is to succeed in erasing oneself so that "one's" Breath-consciousness can establish the desired bond.

Do you think this is possible while seeking to surpass yourself? This is one of the most insidious traps.

Shakyamuni's rejection of asceticism warns of this trap. The boat that enabled one to cross the river must be abandoned on the other bank, otherwise it becomes a burden. But it is still necessary to make the crossing.

Through these descriptions, we can see the similarity between the work of sound, respiration and movement. All three make it possible to guide the "Breath" throughout the body, to make it, just as one knees dough, more fluid, for it to one day become etheric.

It is thanks to this fluidity that the body becomes "permeable" and allows the Spirit to commune with the "undifferentiated breath", which is also consciousness and thus "undifferentiated consciousness".

There is no difference between the Tools offered. Just as with the notion of God, the Tao, the All, the One, the differences expressed often reflect the limits of understanding of the person expressing them.

We have always been astonished by the skepticism of people who, practicing one of the tools mentioned, question the existence of the "tangible presence of the Breath" within the individual. For them, these are metaphors, images, legends. Is this to escape the disappointment of not perceiving it, an impulse of the ego, of the Persona, forgetting, however, that any rejection limits the mind, as well as any evolving perception?

The very essence of the consciousness of the "Breath" is found in prayer, as well as in meditation, because the subtlety of the work makes the approach more difficult. It could be said that the tools for guiding the "Breath" allow a more progressive "presence", while prayer and meditation work more towards "immediateness", but wanting to differentiate the tools seems to us to be a mistake.

In any case, over time, the "Breath" can become present in every action, every thought, every perception. In a word, the "Breath" will become "spirit", the "spirit" will be "Breath", the "Breath" will be consciousness, a new "state of being".

This is what the Sufi Masters lead their disciples toward when saying that the "Dhikr of the Heart" must become a permanent state, like a second breathing or breathing of the Spirit. The same remark could be made about the Orthodox "prayer of the Heart" or the Sikh tradition:

"Why are you printing designs on these sheets, and not focusing your consciousness on the Lord?[1]"

And, one day, it might be able to join the "primordial breath", according to one's destiny.

All authentic traditions have this vocation, and choosing one of them falls to the Seeker, who must then become a "wayfarer".

---

1. Guru Granth Sahib, ang 1375

In Conclusion

Becoming a "wayfarer" and no longer a "Seeker" is a major undertaking... Not because one has reached some goal, but because the path to follow has been found.

All too often, the Seeker becomes lost, tirelessly searching in different doctrines, in initiatory or esoteric groups, for the new and miraculous solution that will magically produce the transformation enabling him to reach a supra-human dimension. Over time, as the miracle fades, all that remains is the intellectual interest of discovering new texts, unknown theories, secret techniques and methods, interesting initiations, leading to the common confusion between culture and the transmutation of being.

Should we remind the principles underlying this confusion?

- *In the first case*, the direction provided is within the limits of the habitual consciousness. Limits of the "classical" senses: we talk, we touch — *the stone, the symbol, etc.*, we feel, hear — *incense, bell, words, music, songs...*, we see — *attitude, outfits, group, ritual*, we taste — *wine, water, Host*, in summary, everything that is within the "usual" perception.

  Of course, emotion can be present, for a whole set of reasons, such as egregore, communion, hysteria, sadness, joy, all influencing the Limbic brain and therefore your conditioning — strengthening the existing conditioning, or setting up a new structure, or making you believe in your spiritual evolution.

  But all of these cannot get you out of your common nature because the elements that make up your quest are of the same "format" as the principles instilled from childhood. "I want — *willpower, a defined objective;* inside a recognized structure — *gregarious, societal;* to achieve results — *I expect a "human" sign — appearance, speech, touch, health, fortune, power;*

or supra-human—*awakening according to the doctrine, to be chosen according to the texts.*" The foundations and structure of your house are therefore strengthened.

Moreover, you cannot but be fully convinced by the principles applied. Why?

Because according to your own intellectual analysis, based itself on your conditioning, this is true, logical, reasonable.

- *In the second case*, it is totally different. Here, we have to remind some notions: it is not a question of accepting some theory—*unity, awakening, union with God*. In this case, this would only be a beautiful reasoning, which would flatter you because of its particularism, making you different from the others, from the ordinary. Here we find those who leave one religion for another or who move into exoticism.

No, it is the opposite:

It is about moving towards the unknown, the unfathomable, the unperceived, the void, the nothingness.

Deep down inside, you feel something that evokes the image of a tiny ember still alive in a fire you thought had gone out. At first, choosing a direction is impossible: without support, without thinking, without reference.

This is the allegory used in the "introduction" indicating that it is necessary to:

- enter the water to where you can still touch the bottom—*if the desire exists, which is not common.*
- then swim without straying too far from the shore—*one must know how to swim first; a "bit" of fear, there is no footing but the landmarks are there, one can be rescued by those who are on the shore.*
- then accept to go farther, without being able to see the shore—*fear, no more references, loneliness.*
- and finally accept to drown—*against one's nature.*

This is found in most dynamic religions, but it is still necessary to hear it and understand it.

It requires work with the appropriate Tool without defining any desired or desirable result—*more power, closer to God, more awake, more than more, more than oneself*—the anchor is then set.

Non nothing, extend towards, do not want, but accept, open all your pores, awaken all your senses and even beyond, but without "force"—*willpower, "habitual" effort*.

And above all, do not expect to feel what someone else has described, felt or "achieved", or what the texts have said, or what your dreams have told you.

Why? Because you are going to think about it, and "every thought leads back to you and closes you off". Also, because your goal can only be within the limits of your existing field of consciousness, so not much. What is more, do not forget that all expression is limited by words, by your understanding, by what can be "brought back" from an experience that goes beyond the limits of the recipient's understanding.

You must strive for the unknown, by accepting not to know, but with total confidence. To take this path of spiritual evolution which must pass from self-centering to allocentrism, you must "become smaller to grow", as described a thousand times in ancient traditions. A paradox incomprehensible by logic alone, but fundamental to any initiatory journey.

The ancient English Bibles used the term "*charity*", not in the sense of charity towards the poorest, to achieve well-being, especially egocentric, but in the sense of "love". Not selfish love infused with the fear of losing the "object" of one's love, but love-empathy where the suffering of the other is one's own, not one's own to bring back to oneself, but one's own because the world suffers, not the philosophical world but the sensitive one made of a universal vibration.

"Forgetting" oneself to the point where the existential being is threatened in its deepest, most essential entity, to the point where the vital essence that supports one's own existence and spirit are threatened to disappear to reach, perhaps, the universal spirit through one's own extinction.

Is it any wonder then:

That the seat of Atman is in the heart, that the symbol of charity and Jesus is the heart, that the representations of Christ Pantocrator is with a mudra closing "the vein of the heart", that "the place where Allah looks" is the heart, that the secret Dhikr is that of the heart (adh-dhikru-l-qalbî), that the seat of the "true Breath" (Zhenqi) is located in the median cinnabar field near the heart, that the most widespread Buddhist sutra is that of the heart?

It is certainly possible that this transition from self-centeredness to allocentrism leads to true "union" love, where any act is really free, where any gain of any kind is futility.

What are we looking for in the work with the tool, in this opening to the "outside", in this relationship with the "object", in the search for "letting go", if not this allocentrism that offers us the opportunity to extract ourselves from our crust?

But make no mistake, this "ideal" state, allowing the much desired union, can only be intermittent. This temporary absolute must not give us the illusion that man then escapes his relative dimension.

The tranquility of the "moment" of union is obviously not present in everyday life. This is made clear by Jesus before his crucifixion: "My God, my God, why have you forsaken me?"

Parable corresponding to the abandonment of the union that precedes the torture of the cross. The symbol of the cross, which recalls the separation felt by the recipient between verticality, the Absolute, where everything is absorbed by it (nothing is important, everything is illusion, everything is one, everything is God) and everyday life, i.e. horizontality, where increasing empathy means that suffering exists, as does the relative dimension of humans.

Nevertheless, such an experience can only lead to a change in the field of consciousness. A definite transformation, but not a metamorphosis, with the exception of a few very rare chosen ones. The absolutes of the human dimension are, unfortunately, often only roles played by actors who meet the criteria of the media and stereotyped appearance. "*Omnia Vanitas*" remains the key word for the human condition.

This last point about human vanity is certainly the trap into which any Seeker can fall. We will not repeat the common ones, such as the desire to appear and to have power, as they are so obvious, yet so insidious; vanity is often hidden behind philanthropic claims. Similarly, our own vanity can lead us to seek, not to merge with the Divine, with the Tao, but to escape our own mediocrity. It is very difficult to discern one's innermost motivation: are we completely sincere with ourselves? The answer is not obvious, as the plank in one's eye is rarely visible.

"Why do you look at the speck of sawdust in your brother's eye and pay no attention to the plank in your own eye? How can you say to your brother, "Let me take the speck out of your eye", when all the time there is a plank in your own eye?[1]*"*

It is important, at every moment, to repel all vanity, which is very difficult for human beings, to say the least. An effective way of doing this is given in the Gospel of Thomas, when Jesus says: *"Be passers-by"*. Indeed, awareness of the ephemerality of all things, including oneself, is essential to suppress any hint of pride. But as always, it is much easier to philosophize on the subject than to become aware of it. Here again, the tool can help, but induction must be given, as always. Thus, every moment of one's life must be experienced in its changing, temporary, transitory aspect.

It makes sense then to take into consideration these two paradoxical dimensions:

- the first dimension, *which one cannot get rid of, except occasionally, in a moment of fusion, of union*, is that of a human, of a creature animated by an overdeveloped ego and a vigilant and omnipresent survival instinct.
- Contrary to what we are led to believe by the reflections of the pseudo-awakened and those closest to God that flourish on the covers of magazines and books.
- the second dimension escapes the first one and is totally unknown to the individual. It corresponds to one's undivided essence, which we could call a "hidden reality". It opposes the first one since it attacks the ego and the instinct of individuality — *a deliberate distinction.*

  It is possible to make an analogy of the "Mohammedan reality" with that of the "cosmic Christ", or with the "nature of Buddha".

If one remains in the first dimension, then it is all about "material" fulfillment, powers, "appearance", super powers, dreams. There is "nothing" to be found — *or almost, but that is "another story"* — because the mystical path is not made to satisfy this dimension, it even "antagonizes" it.

---

1. Matthew 7

That is why, just as a child becomes an adult, there comes a time when it is essential to reject the "Disneyland-esque tales and legends" of esotericism, of initiatory and religious traditions. Detaching oneself from these can be traumatic, and it is not at all certain that every individual can emerge unscathed, or even emerge at all, as this shelter is too comfortable.

However, if one feels a "call of the Profound", free of any preconception, and if the door opens, this "nothing" then comes to life in a new dimension that is beyond ordinary consciousness. On return, the recipient rediscovers his nature, with its various limits—*all the more perceptible as the field of consciousness has widened*—with its ephemerality, illusions and sensitivities that the allocentrism has exacerbated.

So, *what is left?*

A notion of God, Tao, Awakening, which is not "human" but can be lived, an absolute that does not consider individuality, a paradoxical double reality, a nostalgia for the moment of omnipresent fusion.

With this type of approach any hint of vanity evaporates and the Seeker, with a capital S, becomes a humble wayfarer with "the Breath" as the only source from which to drink.

This is our final wish for this shared journey.

There are days whose monotonous length is a pleasure.

Without expectation, without desire.

A languor bathing in softness and tranquility.

Why wish, desire or become?

A God, an awakening, an immanence or a transcendence, what for?

It will happen whether one wants it or not, there is no choice to be made.

No aggression, no noise, a part of the world has fallen asleep, my mind relaxes, not coming, not going, softly suspended, not fighting, forgetting, absorbed and merged, idle soul.

The past is a wave that fades softly, the difficulties seep into the sand, the joys are the sunset.

The sea breeze is a gentle touch that purifies me and my thoughts are blown away. Before yesterday, yesterday, this pointless fight with force and energy, was it useful or even necessary?

Did I want it or was it simply the current that carried me?

The candle trembles, its light fades, a light blow could extinguish it, absence or infinity?

*The child blows
and the soap bubbles fly away
Some burst immediately,
others far away,
Some are round, others deformed,
But they all end up disappearing.
Did they really exist?*

Bibliography

- The Tanakh
- The Bible
- The Quran
- The Guru Granth Sahib
- Tao Te Ching

- Baryosher-Chemouny (Muriel), *La Quête de l'immortalité en Chine*, Éditions Dervy, 1996
- Bergson (Henri), *Spiritual Energy: Essays and Lectures*, 1919
- *The two sources of morality and religion*, University of Notre Dame Press, 1977
- Borel (Henri), *L'esprit de la Chine*, La main courante, 2007
- Dalai Lama and Sheng Yen, Meeting of minds, Dharma Drum Publications, 1999
- Dawkins (Richard), *The Selfish Gene*, OUP Oxford, 2016
- Durckheim (Karlfried Graf), *Courrier du Livre*
- Ehrman (Bart), *Lost Christianities*, Oxford University Press, 2005
- Gardner (Howard), *Multiple intelligences, new horizons*, Basic Books, 2006
- Gandhi, *La Jeune Inde*, translated by Hélène Hart, Librairie Stock, 1925
- Giraud (Daniel), *Seng T'san: Hsin Hsin Ming*, Arfuyen Edition, 1992
- Hui Neng, *The Platform Sutra of the Sixth Patriarch*, Columbia University Press, 1967
- Jung (Carl), *Two essays on analytical psychology*, Collected Works, Vol. 7, Princeton University Press, 1967

- *Man and his symbols,* Dell Publishing Co., 1968
- *Archetypes and the Collective Unconscious (Collected Works of C.G. Jung),* Bolingen Foundation, 1981
- Laborit (Henri), *Éloge de la fuite,* Édition Gallimard, 1993
- Lorenz (Konrad), *Evolution and Modification of Behaviour*
- *On Aggression, Routledge,* 2002
- Maalouf (Amin), *Les croisades vues par les Arabes,* J'ai lu, 1999
- MacLean Paul D., *The Triune Brain in Evolution: Role in Paleocerebral Functions,* Plenum, 1990
- Matringe (Denis), excerpt from the article *"L'Âdi Granth et Gurû Nânak",* Le Point Références, April 2012
- Metanoïa, *Gospel according to Thomas,* Éditions Dervy, 1990
- Moatty (Yves), *Kabir: le fils de Ram et d'Allah,* Éditions Les deux Océans, 1988
- Nyanatiloka (compiler, translator), *The Word of the Buddha: An Outline of the Teaching of the Buddha in the Words of the Pali Canon,* 14th edition, Buddhist Publication Society, 1967
- Prémare (Alfred Louis de), *Les collections de l'Histoire,* 2006
- Renou (Louis), Jean Filliozat, *L'inde classique. Manuel des études indiennes,* A. Maisonneuve, 1991
- Riffard (Pierre), *Ésoterisme d'ailleurs,* Éditions Robert Laffont, 1997
- Shah (Idries), *Wisdom of the idiots—Sufi Stories,* E.P. Dutton and Co., 1971
- Takuan, *Mystère de la sagesse immobile,* Shibata, Albin Michel 1987
- Vivenza (Jean Marc), *Le dictionnaire de René Guénon,* Le Mercure Dauphinois, 2002

- *Hsin Hsin Ming,* English translation by Master Shen Yen
- *Kabir,* translation from Hindi and notes by Charlotte Vaudeville, Oxford: Clarendon Press, 1974
- *Songs of Kabir,* The Macmillan Company, 1915

- *The Bijak of Kabir*, translated by Linda Hess and Shukdeo Singh
- *The book of Chuang Tzu*, translated by Martin Palmer, Penguin Classics, 2006
- *The Complete Works of Zhuangzi*, Columbia University Press, 2013
- *The sacred books of the East (The Tao Teh King)*, translated by James Legge, 1891

- *"My American Uncle"*, a film by based on the works of Henri Laborit, 1980

Discovery Publisher is a multimedia publisher whose mission is to inspire and support personal transformation, spiritual growth and awakening. We strive with every title to preserve the essential wisdom of the author, spiritual teacher, thinker, healer, and visionary artist.

www.ingramcontent.com/pod-product-compliance
Lightning Source LLC
Chambersburg PA
CBHW010045090426
42735CB00018B/3390